BRAVELIVER

BRAVELIVER

A Bipolar Guide To Working In Seattle

JAY CRAIG

Kenneth Craig Publishing Co

For Elmer

The beginning of the pandemic marked the end of my career as Captain Braveliver. Since then I have been constantly looking for my Last Great Job that, with any luck, I will get before I'm too old to work.

Being a Duck Captain was perfect for me because it gave me both a creative outlet to satisfy my manic energy and a lively atmosphere surrounded by fun people that helped stave off depression. Losing that job wasn't just a bummer, it was also kinda scary. People with bipolar disorder have a lower life expectancy than others and I wasn't sure I had the energy or the will to survive what might be coming.

So I hunkered down and bought an old Uhaul to convert into a tiny house to cut my expenses. And I've learned a couple things about managing my manic depression and while not everything is applicable to everybody, it may be more helpful than some book written by a PHD who only knows what crazy people like us tell them. There are many medications out there (some of which are useful, I take lithium, myself) but the fact that I've never had psychiatrists agree on which meds I should be on just tells me that nobody really knows what the hell is going on and the bipolar person is mostly on their own to figure it all out.

But there is one thing that will always be a constant in my life and that is work. Living with bipolar disorder requires hard work, each and every day. There is no Happy Retirement from being bipolar, it is something you will work on the rest of your life.

SHOWER, BED, DISHES

I do three things everyday, no matter what- I take a shower, I make my bed first thing in the morning, and I make sure there are no dirty dishes in the sink when I go to bed.

Doing these three things won't stave off depression but they will lessen it. I don't debate whether or not I'm gonna take a shower, I just do it. I don't ever have a sink full of dirty pans and dishes because I clean things as I go and I learned long ago not to have any extra utensils or glassware, anyway. And there's a reason the military makes their recruits make their beds first thing in the morning- it gives them a sense of accomplishment and provides a sense of order so that no matter what happens during the day they come back to a made bed.

There are other methods of dealing with bipolar disorder, of course, but these three things-

Take a Shower
Make the Bed
Do the Dishes

when done EVERYDAY, will help reduce your depressive episodes.

There are many other things I've learned I need to do to shorten and minimize my manic and depressive episodes but no matter what state of mind I'm in or where I find myself, I start the day with a sense of order and no stink of depression.

Shower. Bed. Dishes.

BUILDING SEATTLE

When Seattle was ravaged by the Great Fire of 1889, it made news all over the country. People were stunned by the photos of the devastation to this little lumber town they'd never heard of, somewhere in the upper left hand corner of the country.

Seattle was beginning to prosper, thanks in large part to the lumber industry, and was ready to seize the opportunity to rebuild the city properly. Their new buildings would be fire resistant and, to solve the problem of having built the initial city on a tidal flat that flooded out twice a day, they would raise the streets and the first floors of Pioneer Square ten to twenty feet.

Just a year later, people across the world started seeing pictures of these beautiful, massive buildings rising up out of the ashes and were amazed at how fast this podunk town was able to rebuild. About one hundred stone and brick buildings went up in less than two years, most of them in the Victorian and Romanesque Revival style. So many that it became the largest collection of Romanesque Revival buildings in the world. It made a huge impression, so when the Klondike Gold Rush hit just eight years later in 1897, Seattle was ready and able to capitalize on it.

The Seattle Chamber of Commerce bought newspaper ads all over the country and people remembered this once tiny lumber town that had burned down and rebuilt almost overnight. Tens of thousands of first-time prospectors flooded into the city and

Seattle's ready merchants sold them everything they could possibly need and then some.

This drawing shows the Pioneer Building on the right and the Starr-Boyd building on the left. The Pioneer Building was named the Finest Building West of Chicago by the American Institute of Architects when it was completed and the asymmetrical Starr-Boyd was designed for two owners who couldn't agree on what the building should look like.

These buildings and a full HALF of the one hundred or so beautiful buildings that went up immediately after the Great Fire were built by the greatest Seattle architect you've probably never heard of, Elmer Fisher.

VIEW OF FRONT STREET LOOKING NORTH FROM YESLER AVENUE.

ELMER FISHER

I was sitting on hold in the Duck Nest one day and looking through some books on Seattle. My tour was pretty heavy on the history and light on the goofiness, and based on the reviews I got on Tripadvisor, people either loved it or hated it. I gave the tour I would want because if I ever had to take a duck tour and was told to play along to some 'YMCA' bullshit I would demand my money back on the spot. So I was always looking for interesting and ironic stories that would be fun to tell.

That's when I discovered Elmer Fisher. It was only a couple paragraphs in some book of odd facts about the State of Washington, I think, but it was all I needed. I did a little research online and printed something out that I taped to the front page of my newspaper just as I got called down to run a tour. I practiced what I was gonna say on the ride down to the ticket booth and contemplated pulling over on one of the side streets off First Avenue because my Pioneer Square history was too heavy as it was. I was already driving too slow and purposely hitting the lights for more time, giving my guests more history than they could ever hope to retain and locals yet another reason to hate us.

I always went as far South as I could before turning into Pioneer Square to give me more time but since I was now gonna pull over for five minutes I decided to pull onto Main Street, right in the heart of the old neighborhood. Turned out that this was a perfect place to sit and shove some facts and stories down the throats of my paying tourists.

On the first tour of my new route I stopped at a place where other drivers could get around me, cut the engine and set the brake. As I was getting out of my chair to deliver my new presentation of the history of Seattle, I noticed something cool.

"You see that wall there, behind that dumpster?" I made a quick look to the other side of the street to see if there was something else to talk about in case on the next tour there might be a homeless person taking a dump there. "You see how there's kind of an arch in the bricks right there above the pavement? See how it's just like the arch over the first floor window? What's that all about, right?" Everybody seemed interested, so far.

"It's because that first floor window was originally the second floor window and that partially submerged arch below it used to be over what was the actual first floor window!" I then went into the whole story about how Seattle was built on a tidal flat between a forest of old growth trees and a deep water port to ship out all that lumber. But the place was kind of a dump. It would flood out every time there was a high tide and the sewer lines would back up into people's houses.

"So when the city burned to the ground in 1889, the business and civic leaders got together and decided to rebuild the city and this time they were gonna do it right. They agreed they would raise the city and build a seawall to keep the water out and make all the new buildings out of brick, stone and steel. No more wood. They had money now because they were a lumber town and San Francisco, Seattle's biggest customer, kept burning down because they kept rebuilding out of wood. Seattle even formed a Building and Loan they named Washington Mutual to help finance the whole thing."

Since I was turned around and facing my guests, I could read their interest level. They were looking at me and smiling so I would continue with the long version. If they had quackers in their mouths or were talking to each other, they would have gotten the short version.

"Where we're sitting right now used to be about ten or fifteen feet lower. So what they did was come up with some rules about how all these new buildings were gonna be built. First rule- no more wood! San Francisco can keep burning down if they want but this was gonna be Seattle's last fire so all new buildings must be made out of brick, stone and steel.

"Second rule was that all these new buildings must have a store-front on the second story 'cause the plan was that they would build all these new buildings and then the city would raise the streets ten or fifteen feet to the height of the second floors. Then they would build sidewalks from the new elevated streets to the new second floors. Problem solved!

"Well, the buildings went up fast. Amazingly fast. About one hundred buildings in less than a year and a half, which is amazing, considering how beautiful they are. And the streets went up fast, too. Once the buildings were up the City came in and they put a ten to fifteen foot wall on one side of the original street, same thing on the other side, filled in between with dirt, and then laid cobble-stones on top and Boom!, instant elevated street.

"The problem was the sidewalks. They never really hashed out who was gonna pay for the sidewalks, the business owners or the City, so for years there were no sidewalks. If you wanted to cross the street you had to climb a twenty foot ladder, walk across this new elevated street, and then down another twenty foot ladder. Nobody died in the fire but something like seventeen people died from falling off the new roads or from walking on the original side-walks and having a horse and carriage fall off the new road and kill 'em. It was crazy!"

Depending on how interested they looked, I'd go into the Underground and Beneath the Streets tours and other things to see in Pioneer Square. And then it was time to try out my new favorite topic- Elmer Fisher.

"You see that big, beautiful building right there, that one with the stone and arches and all that?", I asked, pointing to whatever cool building was closest. "That style of architecture is called Richardsonian Romanesque Revival and it was designed by a guy named Elmer Fisher.

"Elmer Fisher was a Scotsman. He was born in Edinburgh and came to the United States as a young man. He worked his way across the country as a carpenter and landed in Seattle just a little bit before the Great Fire in 1889. The very first newspaper that came out had a big ad, right on the front page that said 'ELMER FISHER, ARCHITECT!!', and talked about how he went to the finest architectural college and worked in the best architectural firms," I held up my newspaper that I had taped a piece of paper on that said, 'ELMER FISHER, ARCHITECT!! BLAH BLAH BLAH!!', as if to prove it.

"Elmer got the jobs to design over FIFTY of the hundred or so buildings that went up within a year and a half of the fire. He chose the Romanesque Revival style developed by Henry Richardson of the Chicago School, if you know what that is, and all the other local architects did the same style so it was the largest collection of Romanesque Revival buildings anywhere in the world. And while all the architects are doing two or three buildings and Elmer's doing over FIFTY! It's amazing!"

At this point I'd get back in my seat, start the engine and crawl up to the intersection and purposely hit the light. "See that building across the street there, on the corner?", I asked, pointing to the Romanesque Revival building at the corner of First and Main. That's also one of Elmer's! Isn't it beautiful? And see those stairs in the sidewalk that go down to the original first floor? They go down to a coffee shop that was the inspiration for that TV show Frasier. Anybody know the name of that coffee shop?"

If somebody yelled, 'Cafe Nervosa!', I'd slow down and block traffic so they could get a picture. I could expect about thirty to forty dollars in tips per tour and that was an added five bucks from at least one middle aged couple. I learned later that it wasn't actually one of Elmer's buildings but in all fairness, of the fifty buildings that Elmer built in Pioneer Square, there are only about a dozen left and you could only see half of them on our route.

As I turned onto First Avenue I realized the timing was perfect and I ended up doing this exact tribute to Elmer probably another two thousand times. "See that gray building there? That's one of Elmer's! (It wasn't.) And this one here! How cool is this building with all the rusticated stone?" (I had just learned the term 'rusticated stone' and was starting to show off.)

By now I was randomly pointing at every cool looking building with rusticated stone. "Elmer designed this building and that building and not only did he design all these buildings, but he also oversaw their construction! Imagine designing and overseeing the construction of FIFTY buildings in just a year and a half!", I said, slowly rolling up First. As we got to the intersection of First and Yesler I was relieved to not be talking about Skid Road and happy to be drawing people's attention to something that actually matters.

I made sure to catch the light because there was so much to talk about here. "These two buildings on our left are Elmer's (true), and the one across the street with the toy store in it (actually also one of Elmer's, it turns out). And on the other side see that god awful parking garage there? They call it the Sinking Ship. Well, it used to be the Hotel Seattle, and it was considered the finest hotel on the West Coast when it was built. It was a flatiron and a very high-end hotel. It fell into disrepair in the fifties and they tore it down in the early sixties, which pissed off so many people they formed a Preservation District to save the rest of the buildings. That's another one of Elmer's. (Not really, but they got the point.)"

I inched through the intersection and stopped in front of the plaza that's the official center of Pioneer Square. I didn't have time to talk about the pergola or the totem pole because motorists are touchy enough as it is.

"Okay, get your cameras out, people!" People need to be told what's picture-worthy, I found. "That right there is the Pioneer Building! Pretty amazing, right? It's the most beautiful building in Seattle, and who made it?"

"ELMER FISHER!", they yelled.

"Damn right he did! And when it was done it was named the Finest Building West of Chicago by the American Institute of Architects. It's my favorite building in Seattle, get a good picture!

"Elmer Fisher designed and oversaw the construction of at least FIFTY buildings that all went up in less than two years! Well, they looked into it a couple years after he died and discovered that Elmer Fisher wasn't from Scotland, never went to college, and never worked for any architectural firms. He just read a lot of books and looked at pictures in magazines! And he created the Finest Building West of Chicago! Yaaay!!! There's a lesson in there somewhere, kids, but I'll let you and your parents figure that one out."

I quit Ride the Ducks when they told me to tone down the history and start doing some quacking games because some people, apparently, just wanted to drive around Seattle like a bunch of idiots quacking at people on the sidewalk like it's the funniest thing they've ever done. And some of these same people complained that they were told they had to buy a Wacky Quacker for $2.50 because we were gonna be doing 'Quacking Games' and they wouldn't want to be left out. And then they'd get on my Duck and part of my intro would be how much I hated those quackers and to put them away, because they're souvenirs, and you know what you do with a souvenir? "YOU PUT IT IN YOUR POCKET TIL YOU GET HOME!!!", I would yell. I had a great tour and there was no way I was gonna share it with a fucking plastic novelty toy.

But I never forgot about Elmer Fisher and over the years I've searched for any information about him that I could find, which has always been frustratingly sparse. I'm convinced he was bipolar, and for years I've been looking for evidence of it, as if I need it. You know how gay people have 'gaydar' and just know when someone else is gay? I've been dealing with Bipolar Disorder my whole adult life and I can spot another bipolar person faster and more accurately than any professional in the mental health field. I don't know anything about any of the other mental illnesses, but Bipolar Disorder (aka Manic Depression, aka Scottish Buddhism), that I know.

There's no point in debating whether or not Elmer was bipolar. He was. More important to me is his contribution to the development of Seattle, which has been widely overlooked. Elmer was certainly well-regarded during his short career, but it was his buildings and influence on other architects that the Seattle Chamber of Commerce used to promote Seattle as the jumping off point to Alaska during the Klondike Gold Rush of 1897. If it wasn't for Elmer's work, it's very likely the prospectors would have just gone to San Francisco or Vancouver to get outfitted.

In the five years between 1886 and 1890 when he was active in the Pacific Northwest, Elmer designed at least eighty commercial buildings, residences and churches. That's an average of over fifteen buildings a year, which is amazing. I looked at other architects of the time and couldn't find any that averaged over three buildings a year making Elmer Fisher, by my account, anyway, the most prolific architect of his time. By far.

·BURKE'S·BLOCK·SECOND·STREET·

ELMER FISHER
CURRICULUM VITAE

I was born in Edinburgh, Scotland in 1840 to Horace and Lucy Fisher. I moved to the United States at age seventeen to pursue a career in architecture. I took a break from my education to fight in the War Between the States for the 21st Infantry Regiment. We fought valiantly in the Battles of Antietam and Fredericksburg, and the Second Battle of Bull Run, though I prefer not to talk about it.

I finished my education at a very prominent architectural college and worked for several notable architectural firms, too numerous to bother mentioning.

I began my solo career in Vancouver, British Columbia, directly after the Fire of 1886, wherein I built Vancouver's first fireproof hotel, the Byrnes Building, which I am sure you have heard of. I followed that with fifteen more buildings in Victoria and then six more in Port Townsend before expanding to Seattle.

On June 6th of 1889, fire erupted two blocks from my architectural offices and although I was able to save a number of buildings upwind, almost the entire downtown was destroyed. I almost single-handedly led the Reconstruction of Seattle that saw over one hundred buildings constructed in about a year and a half. I chose the style of HH Richardson's dynamic Romanesque Revival while humbly making it my own.

With the wild success I enjoyed, I then took a break from my labors and sought adventure in the Klondike Gold Rush.

I am now re-establishing my architectural career here in Los Angeles and I expect great things from this city. Cheers!

PIONEER·BLOCK·CORNER·FRONT·AND·JAMES·STREETS·

THE PIONEER BUILDING

1889-1891

This representation of the Pioneer Building is what was called a Presentation Drawing. When a property owner wanted to construct a new building he or she would either go to an architect they knew or put it out to bid. Prospective architects would submit a presentation drawing and if it were a private owner, that might be enough. If it were a county or school building, for example, several architects would compete against each other and sometimes have to submit multiple designs. Along with the design, the architect would also submit the estimated costs of materials and labor.

Some architects of the time focused on private commissions because there was less hassle to them and some architects preferred going after large scale projects like courthouses and city halls.

Henry Yesler, one of the Founders of Seattle and one of its most influential citizens, decided he wanted a large upscale office building bigger and better than anything Seattle had ever seen. He met Elmer Fisher shortly after Elmer arrived in Seattle and together they came up with a design rich in rusticated sandstone and other elements that would fit right in with Henry Richardson's Romanesque Revival style that came out of Chicago. This would be Elmer's first big commission in Seattle and his first Romanesque Revival building. The first design was much smaller than the current building and they first started digging out the foundation in 1888, the year before the Great Fire. Construction was slow because the cost of such a project was so great.

The Great Fire in the Summer of 1889 suddenly made property in Seattle much more valuable because the timing was right for a massive building boom. Henry Yesler was able to sell off some of his property at top dollar and finance the bigger, better version of the Pioneer Building that we have today.

This building, the Finest Building West of Chicago according to the American Institute of Architects at the time, not only helped set the direction of Seattle's reconstruction, it also placed Elmer Fisher firmly on top of the architects to watch.

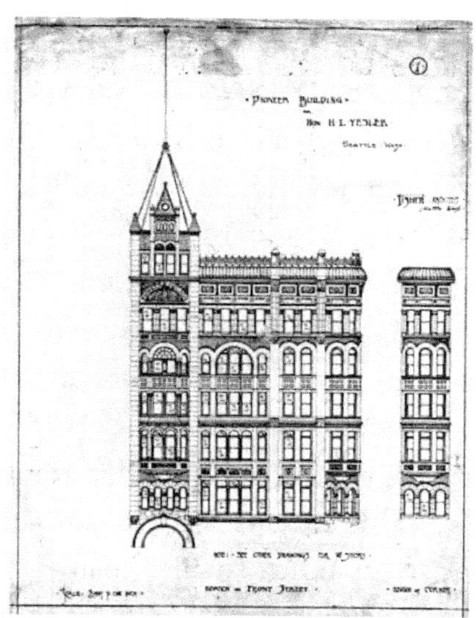

Some of the presentation drawings have remained because they would have been well taken care of, either in a drawer in an architect's office or as a piece of art kept by the building's new owner. The detail drawings, however, were never meant as art. They were meant as instructions for stone masons, bricklayers, carpenters, glaziers, etc, and not many remain because these drawings were taken to the job site and would have just been tossed out afterwards. These drawings are dirty because they were most likely sitting on work tables all over the job site.

An interesting thing about these drawings is that they were most likely meant for the bricklayers doing the upper floors, as the first floor and basement would have already been completed by the stonemasons. Another interesting thing is that the presentation drawing has 'HL Yesler' on the top arch but in the detail drawings, as well as the actual building, it's 'Pioneer Building'.

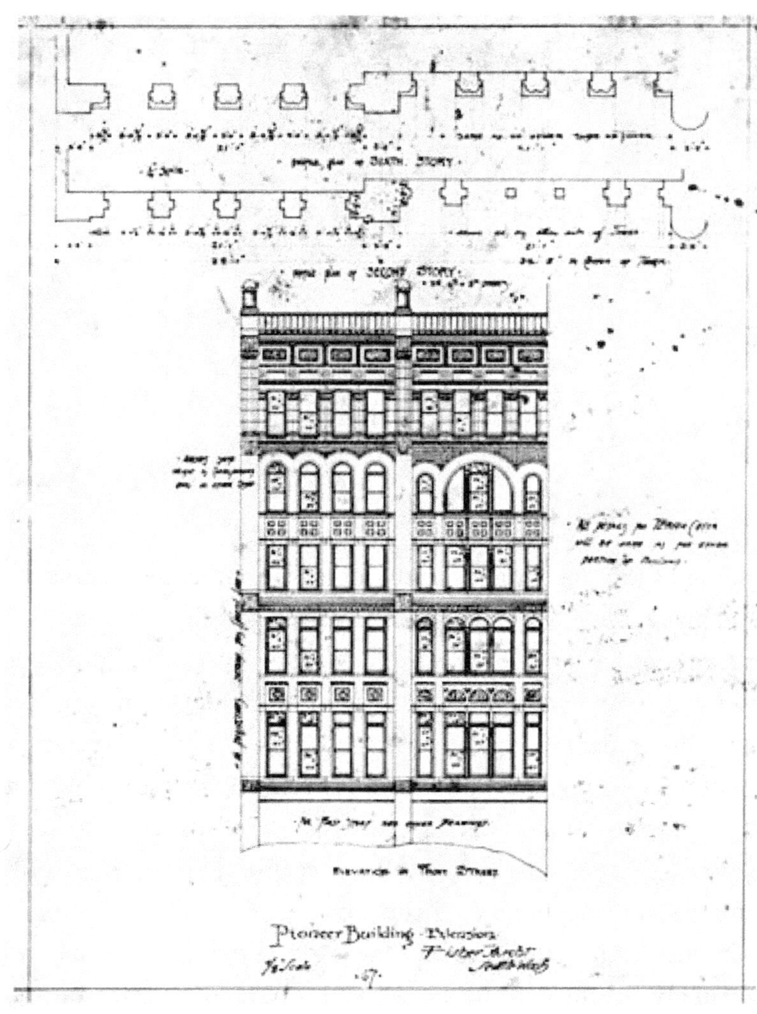
PARTIAL PLAN OF SIXTH STORY
PARTIAL PLAN OF SECOND STORY
ELEVATION ON THIRD STREET
Pioneer Building Extension

IT

Walk through any mental institution and you'll come across dozens of patients who will swear they have a direct connection to God Almighty. Even the much-quoted holy book of Christians, the Bible, is full of people who were completely off their nut but are still revered as saints and prophets. What a world.

Mania-induced euphoria is a wonderful feeling and it's easy to see why a person experiencing IT would automatically assume IT was from the Creator of the Universe ITself. IT is a very physical and real sensation that demands some kind of mental rationalization that for most people can only be explained by a direct connection to some kind of deity. Speaking in tongues, talking to a burning bush, cursing at God for abandoning you on a cross... pure crazy talk that, depending on who said it, has been either glorified or used to incarcerate people.

But that feeling of pure joy and a connection to the universe is very real and when I get IT, IT is wonderful. IT completely makes up for the worst of the worst depression and IT's better than any drug I've ever taken. IT lasts much longer than sex and is worth more than all the money in the world.

Everything makes complete sense when IT hits you and even though IT's impossible to articulate to most people, you can't blame them for not getting IT. So I've learned to accept this and try to keep IT to myself, as much as I can.

I no longer send emails or post things on Facebook or Instagram at two o'clock in the morning and neither should you. What seems like a perfectly rational yet brilliant idea on how to improve your new workplace will absolutely not be taken in the spirit IT was intended, no matter who you send it to. Absolutely DO NOT write an email with the intention of sleeping on IT and sending IT in the morning because you WILL NOT sleep on IT, you will read IT a couple times and send IT off, every time. If you have an Idea that is so Great, sit on IT for a while. IT is likely years ahead of IT's time anyway.

THE BIPOLAR ARCHITECT

Here's what I've come to learn about Elmer H Fisher- He was born in Royalston, Massachusetts in 1851 to Horace and Lucy Fisher. His first recorded job appears to have been as a mechanic in 1873 at age twenty-two and married Mahala Covey that same year. Also that same year he quit his job and moved to Minneapolis and became a cabinetmaker. Two years later he got a job as a sash maker for a well-established window manufacturer and kept that job for an impressive five years before abandoning his wife and moving to Denver to work as a bandsaw operator, and then starting a business as a building contractor. There he met Mary Smith, whom he lived with as husband and wife but couldn't marry because he was still technically married to his first wife, Mahala.

In 1886, at age 35, he and Mary moved to Victoria, BC, where he presented himself as a 46 year-old Scottish architect. And it worked. He probably even took on a Scottish accent and this is where I imagine he first sold himself as an accomplished architect who graduated from an architectural college and worked in the finest architectural firms.

Meanwhile, in the late 1880s, the cities of the Pacific North-west- Seattle, Victoria, Portland, Tacoma, Port Townsend and many others all thought they would be the dominant city. Seattle was already the economic center of the territory due to the lumber industry but the other growing cities hoped they could convince the various railroads to make them their terminus, ensuring they would become Pacific Northwest's major city. Port Townsend was already calling itself the City of Dreams with full expectations of becoming the largest port in the Pacific Northwest.

Elmer took out newspaper ads and in three years he built his first seventeen buildings in Victoria, Vancouver and surrounding areas. One of the first was in the charming Gastown neighborhood of Vancouver. It's called the Byrnes building (1886-1887) and it's still there. It was one of the very first fireproof buildings built after Vancouver's fire of 1886. There are a handful of his buildings still standing but from what I've seen, they are mostly Italianate and Victorian style buildings. After just two years, Elmer was confident enough to open architectural firms in both Port Townsend and Seattle, Washington. He left Mary in Victoria and promised her he would send for her once he established himself.

In February of 1887, he got the job to create the McCurdy building in Port Townsend, his first building in Washington Territory. He also ventured into the booming city of Seattle and with a solid reputation behind him from his work in British Columbia, set up what would become his primary architectural office.

1888 was a busy year for Elmer Fisher. He was still getting large contracts in Victoria, at least five more. But he also built the James and Hastings Building in Port Townsend and got eight building contracts in Seattle. Immediately after the Great Fire of June 1889 he hired four draftsmen and quickly became the dominant architect in Seattle.

People have done more research and even added to Elmer's wikipedia page since I first started talking about him, so my first presentation about him on the Ducks wasn't completely accurate. He did not show up out of nowhere with no experience and build half the buildings after the fire. Instead, he showed up in Victoria out of nowhere with no experience and established himself as a talented and dependable architect before expanding first into Port Townsend and then into Seattle. The fact that he was already established in Seattle before the Great Fire was due more to foresight and intelligence than shit luck.

Shortly after Elmer's arrival in Victoria, the then-much-smaller Vancouver had a massive fire in 1886. One of Elmer's first contracts was to build the George Byrnes Block, which was one of the first fireproof buildings in the area and people took notice. It was no joke that San Francisco kept burning down and they kept rebuilding out of wood or that Seattle was getting rich selling them the lumber. And a quick look around Seattle would tell you this prosperous lumber town, itself made mostly of wood buildings, could very easily burst into flames and be in a position to rebuild quickly. Brick and stone buildings would be the future.

Elmer Fisher may have misrepresented himself but he was no fraud. Elmer was a worker. He taught himself how to construct spectacular buildings that still stand today. He was obviously intelligent, but most importantly he put in the time. Intelligence comes naturally, you either have it or you don't. But some things require massive amounts of diligence and conviction which sometimes can come easier to people who are manic, people who can get so wrapped up in a project there's no turning it off or even setting it aside until it's over.

Most of my manic projects have been utter failures as far as providing any real income goes but they were a great way of burning off energy. I spent thousands of hours developing wildly unique Great Highland bagpipes that I was convinced would change the entire music industry. Nobody had ever made a fully functional Great Highland bagpipe out of green marble, driftwood, or ancient Egyptian hammered bronze, and nobody has certainly ever made a two-man percussion bagpipe. These were fully-functional bagpipes that caught the attention of bagpipers all over the world but instead of getting a single order for a custom bag-pipe, I was mocked and derided for my efforts, which kept my manic episodes somewhat in check. Had I received the proper adulation for figuring out how to make a fucking GREAT HIGH-LAND BAGPIPE out of brass, carbon fiber, fiberglass, and a bunch of other composite materials, and have the sound be PERFECT, which it was, then my manic bagpipe episode would have lasted for years, not just months at a time. Of course, then my crash would have lasted much longer and been much deeper.

Elmer Fisher began his architectural career at the age of thirty-five and by the time he was forty he was responsible for dozens and dozens of iconic buildings around the Pacific Northwest and it I would argue that he was pivotal in Seattle becoming the city it is today. At the height of his career he was fully respected and honored as Seattle's prominent architect and had to turn down jobs constantly.

Very little was written about Elmer Fisher during his lifetime, unfortunately, and of the eighty-five or so buildings that he was responsible for, only about thirty remain. Elmer helped shape Seattle after the Great Fire and was gone in about five years. And if you are in Seattle, Port Townsend and a couple surrounding areas, you can still find some of his work. In Victoria and Vancouver, BC you can see how he started his career as an architect, with a couple Victorian houses and his first brick buildings. In Port Townsend you can see his first large scale business blocks. In Seattle you can see his incredible takes on Richardsonian Romanesque Revival that inspired what would become the largest collection of Romanesque Revival buildings in the world, and he did it in just a few short years.

CHIEF-OF-ALL-WOMEN REPLICA TOTEM POLE

In 1899, the Seattle Chamber of Commerce and the Seattle Post-Intelligencer newspaper organized a Goodwill Committee to visit various Alaskan sites aboard a steamer ship named the City of Seattle. When they got to the Tlingit (pronounced KLING-it) village on Tongas Island, and saw that the village appeared mostly deserted and all the fishing boats were out, their fearless leader, James Clise, instructed a few of his crew to go ashore and grab the biggest totem pole they could find. And quickly, before everybody came back from fishing.

The largest totem pole was built in dedication for a woman who had drowned over a hundred years earlier and was named The Chief-of-All-Women. This was the most sacred totem to the Crow Clan and at 50', towered over the other dozen or so poles. The crew hurriedly chopped down the totem pole, rolled it to the shore while breaking various beaks and wings, and then cut it in two so it could fit on the boat. All of this was witnessed by a couple of village members who were too old and terrified to do anything about it so the crew of the City of Seattle was able to make a leisurely escape. The Tlingit demanded the return of their cherished totem pole (built over a hundred years earlier), or at least some compensation for it. And after a legal settlement for $20,000 was just laughed at by James Clise and the Chamber of Commerce, the Post-Intelligencer made a peace offering of $500. It's not known if that paltry settlement ever made its way to the proper owners of the Chief-of-All-Women but nevertheless it was erected in Pioneer Square and used to promote the successful Alaska-Yukon-Pacific Exposition a few years later.

In 1938, somebody lit the totem pole on fire, damaging the already neglected totem pole beyond repair. Fortunately, the Civilian Conservation Corps was employing Tlingit wood carvers to fix a bunch of other totem poles at the time and Seattle was able to have a brand new replica built in just three months. And because the US Forestry Dept donated the wood and the Tlingits were already getting paid minimum wage, the US Government just handed over the new Chief-of-All-Women totem pole to Seattle at no cost! That's TWO totem poles for the cost of none.

PERGOLA

The pergola in Pioneer Square was built in 1909 and was considered by some to be the Finest Cable Car Stop West of the Mississippi (!), and with its fancy underground bathrooms featuring terrazzo tile, Alaskan marble and polished metal fixtures, it might well have been. Others, however, thought it was a complete waste of money and that there would be no way to maintain it. It would enable homeless people. It was unsightly. It was extravagant. Not in front of my business!

It was called a Comfort Station and for several years it was spectacular, at least as far as public urban toilets go. There were staff to keep the place clean and stocked and within a short time there was talk of similar comfort stations all over the city. The thought of public toilets certainly wasn't original, but neither was the opposition to providing basic services to people. After several years the comfort station gradually lost funding and was closed during WWII to 'ration money for the war effort'.

The underground toilets were closed off for good and the pergola stopped being useful when they got rid of the cable cars. The pergola is made of cast iron and glass and had to be rebuilt when a truck driver took the corner too tight and brought it down in 2001. There's no bus that goes near there now, and apart from offering a little shelter from the rain, its purpose now is strictly ornamental.

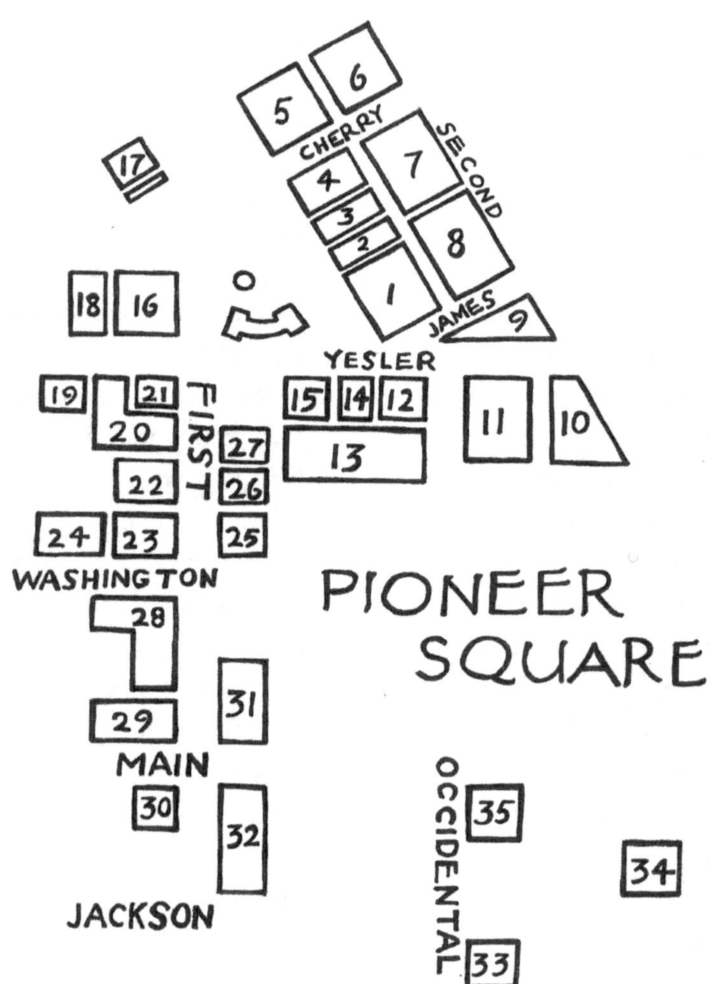

5
6
CHERRY
17
4
SECOND
7
3
2
8
1
18
16
JAMES
9
YESLER
19
21
FIRST
15
14
12
11
10
20
27
13
22
26
24
23
25
WASHINGTON
28
PIONEER
SQUARE
29
31
MAIN
30
32
OCCIDENTAL
35
34
JACKSON
33

[1]

Pioneer Building, Elmer Fisher, 1889

This and the Burke Building were Elmer's most celebrated buildings. Elmer came to Seattle in late 1888 and quickly made a name for himself when he got the commission from Henry Yesler to build the original version of this building before the Great Fire of June 6th, 1889, which must have totally pissed off William Boone, the preeminent Seattle architect of the time. After the fire, Yesler was able to sell some property and finance the larger version that still stands today. This is the building that threw down the gauntlet to all the other architects and made Pioneer Square what it is today. Take in the incredible rusticated Chuckanut sandstone, cast iron bays over the three entrances, and imagine the tower that used to be on top. Or Google it. It's spectacular. Influenced by Henry Hobson Richardson, this is Elmer's most enduring example of Richardsonian Romanesque Revival architecture.

Definitely try to get into this building, if you can. There's a front desk person but they're there mostly to help you find somebody rather than to keep you out. Just say you're looking to rent some space from 'Expansive' but you want to look around a little first. Ride the elevator up and take in the beautiful woodwork and atrium. The architect's job back then was to design the interior as well as the exterior, which just makes the fact that Elmer designed and oversaw the construction of so many buildings in such a short time even more remarkable.

[2]
Howard Building, Elmer Fisher, 1890

Originally called the Tremont Building, there's not a lot of information about this building. But I saw somewhere that it was 'attributed to Elmer Fisher' which is good enough for me. Plus, it totally looks like one of his buildings and it abuts the Pioneer Building so it just makes sense.

A lot of people think the Underground Tour starts in the Pioneer Building but it actually operates out of this one. I love the Underground Tour but as many times as I've taken it, I've never once heard them even mention Elmer Fisher. They go under his buildings almost exclusively and don't seem to have any freaking idea who he was, even though I've tried to tell them many times.

[3]
Lowman and Hanford Building, Emil de Neuf, 1892

Emil de Neuf came over from Germany as a young man with a degree in architecture. Or so he said. He was one of Elmer's four draftsmen between 1889-91, and appears to have been his top draftsman even though he was just in his twenties. When Elmer flamed out in 1891, Emil took over many of his clients and finished much of his work. This building, though, was all Emil and part of the Lowman and Hanford Stationary Empire.

[4]
Lowman Building, Emil de Neuf, 1902

James Lowman came to Seattle at the urging of his uncle, Henry Yesler, in 1877 and did VERY well for himself, as partner in the Lowman and Hanford Stationery & Printing Company, among other things. To design this more modern and less clunky building than all the Romanesque Revival buildings, he turned to Emil and his new partner, Augustus Heide, an itinerant but talented architect, much like Emil and Elmer.

Two of the most influential architects in America were Henry Hobson Richardson and Louis Sullivan, who were among the founders of the Chicago School of Architecture, which was more of a movement than a formal institution. Elmer and most of the other architects took on the Richardsonian Romanesque Revival aesthetic directly after the fire, but afterwards all but Elmer turned to the new and exciting work that Sullivan was doing, which included steel frames and exterior walls that didn't need to be load bearing. This allowed for larger windows and better light, which was more appealing to the building owner and prospective tenants. Note how much more modern and welcoming the storefronts are in this building compared to the others. That's all due to the new steel frame technique.

The storefront on the Southwest corner was home to Utilikilts before the pandemic. When the cruise ships were in town there would be thousands of tourists wandering by and on my days off from the Ducks I would hang out in front of the store with a beer in my hand and get some dude from Texas who's never even seen a non-traditional kilt to come in and drop $250 on a Workman's Utilikilt, usually to the amazement of his wife. The fridge was always stocked with good beer 'cause dropping hundreds of dollars on basically a man-skirt makes much more sense after a couple strong IPAs. The Ducks would drive by several times a day and as I was starting to get shitfaced, the tour guides would stop calling me Captain Braveliver and just call me Jay and treat me like I was just another homeless drunk.

[5]
Sheuerman Building, Elmer Fisher, 1889

Also called the Good Arts building, this building appears to be one of the first of Elmer's to go up after the fire. I see pictures of the area in 1890 and this building is up while it looks like the Pioneer Building is barely started. The dates I'm ascribing to all of the buildings are the earliest dates that I've found because this is more about when the buildings were designed than about when they were finished. Sometimes you'll see conflicting dates for a building because one date is for when construction began and another is for when the building was complete and ready to occupy. And there are a couple buildings that nobody even knows who the architect was because the paperwork has been lost over time.

The upstairs floors are mostly art studios but definitely pop into the Cherry St Coffee House and check it out. I recommend the garlic bagel egg sandwich.

[6]
Hoge Building, Bebb & Mendel, 1909

This building was planned and construction begun at the same time as the Smith Tower. Both buildings were going to be 18 stories but there was a bit of a friendly rivalry going on and John Hoge quietly raised the height of each floor just a little bit. The Hoge Building became Seattle's tallest building for three years- until a massive tower was added to the design of the Smith Building, making it the tallest building on the West Coast when it was completed in 1914. This was also the site of the first wood planked house built in Seattle, by the first Sheriff in town, Carson Boren in 1852.

[7]
Bailey Building, Saunders & Houghton, 1889

This was the first commission for the newly formed Saunders & Houghton Partnership. It was one of the few buildings built entirely of sandstone, in this case Tenino Sandstone from outside Olympia. Most other buildings were using sandstone just for the first floor and basements, and brick for the upper floors and when this, their first building, took a full three years to complete the local paper graciously called its construction 'careful'.

When the sandstone would show up at a job site, it would all be rough cut to approximate size. The local masons would then cut each block to the proper size and smooth out each side except the outward facing side which would remain rough and exaggerated. It was labor intensive but labor was cheap with so many workers pouring into the city seeking work after the Fire.

[8]
Butler Block, John Parkinson, 1890

This building was designed by a young Englishman named John Parkinson who had shown up in the United States just a few years earlier with a reported $5 in his pocket. He initially worked in Elmer's firm in 1889 as a draftsman alongside Emil de Neuf while Emil was 26, John was 28 and Elmer was 38. But if you asked Elmer, he was 49, of course.

This was originally an office building, then called the Butler Hotel, which hosted three presidents, including Teddy Roosevelt. In the 1930s, everything above the second floor was removed and it was converted into a parking garage.

[9]
Sinking Ship (Occidental Hotel, Hotel Seattle,
Stephen Meany, 1889)

This monstrosity, ugly as it is, helped save Pioneer Square. This site was originally home to the Occidental Hotel, a fine luxury hotel that was destroyed in the Fire. It was rebuilt and renamed the Hotel Seattle, also a well-loved upscale hotel. It was designed by Stephen Meany, who also designed the beautifully massive Colman Building at First and Columbia just a couple blocks away. The Colman building has two Irish bars, Fado and the Owl N' Thistle, that are both worth a visit for a quick pint.

The Hotel Seattle was damaged in an earthquake in the 1940s, fell into disrepair, and was demolished without warning in 1961, freaking out people like Victor Steinbrueck, Bill Speidel and many others. The god-ugly Sinking Ship parking garage was built in 1965 and included arched metal tubing that was apparently meant to be reminiscent of the arched doorways and windows of the neighboring buildings. It didn't work. The Pioneer Square Preservation District was formed soon after to make sure something like this would not happen again.

[10]
Metropole Building, Elmer Fisher, Emil deNeuf, 1892 (1890?)

It's believed that Elmer designed this building for Henry Yesler, but he was gone by the time construction began, leaving it to Emil to oversee the project. With all the property and buildings Yesler had going on, it seems this one was put on the back burner for a couple years.

Elmer used mostly Chuckanut sandstone in his buildings and this is one of only a couple that used rusticated stone exclusively, without any brick on the face walls. It's also one of three buildings on this stretch of Yesler Way that are abandoned but still protected from being torn down because they're part of the Pioneer Square Preservation District.

[11]

Seattle National Bank, Interurban Building,
John Parkinson, 1890

This was the building that made John Parkinson. He worked as a draftsman for Elmer for over a year before going out on his own and his first two large commissions were this and the Butler Block. And while the Butler Block was impressive enough, the Seattle National Bank, now called the Interurban building, was built to rival Elmer's Burke Building as the most impressive building in Seattle. I love the detail on the Colorado Sandstone, including the lion's head at the corner entrance. This building seems to get lost in conversations about Seattle's most impressive buildings, but notice the rounded brick columns. I think it's one of the coolest buildings of that time.

After this building, Parkinson designed the BF Day school, and then was appointed to be the Architect and Superintendent of Seattle Schools. In 1894, after losing his job and investments because of the Panic of '93, he relocated to Los Angeles and was responsible for some of that city's finest and most enduring buildings, including the LA Coliseum and the LA City Hall. He was the most successful architect to come out of the Seattle Fire. And he must have felt grateful to Elmer to some degree because he hired him to be his office manager in the last two troubled years of Elmer's life.

[12]
Korn Building #2, Elmer Fisher, 1889

This is one of the first buildings erected after the fire and was actually a replacement to the Korn Building #1 that Elmer also designed upon setting up an office in Seattle in December of 1888, before being destroyed in the fire. It was built for one of Seattle's founders, Charles Terry but named for Moses Korn who operated a drug store on the first floor. I'm pretty sure the top floors were originally a hotel but this building was abandoned many years ago.

[13]
Walker Building, William Boone, 1891

This building was built for Cyrus Walker, a successful lumberman who also commissioned William Boone to build the beautiful Globe Building, among others. This building was supposed to be four stories but for whatever reason it never got past the first floor. It's now called the Al & Bob's Saveway Building.

[14]
Eagle Cafe, Elmer Fisher, 1890

Many times, two buildings would go up and there would be a space in between that needed to be filled. The Eagle Cafe was a 'filler building' and it's possible that Elmer might have let one of his draftsmen have a go at it. It's more likely to me that Elmer was more supportive of his proteges than threatened by them so it's quite possible he would have let them design some of the smaller buildings.

[15]
Merchants Cafe, William Boone, 1889

William Boone was the most prolific Seattle architect before Elmer Fisher came along. Boone built Henry Yesler's huge and opulent mansion that was so big it would be used as Seattle's first public library after Henry Yesler's death. He designed the massive New York Building that was considered one of the greatest buildings in the city. Boone had a long and prosperous career in Seattle and was still designing buildings at 75 years old. He helped form the Washington State branch of the American Institute of Architects and was very active in the Chamber of Commerce. In total, William Boone designed about 53 buildings in 22 years. Of course, Elmer Fisher did that many in a year and a half, but the comparison is unfair- William Boone did not have the benefit of being manic. He did, however, lead a happy life and live into his 90's.

The Merchants Cafe opened in 1890 and has stayed in business all that time, making it the oldest operating restaurant in Seattle (don't order the shrimp). Stop in for some food and a beer and definitely go downstairs where you can stand underneath the sidewalk and get a real understanding of how they raised the city after the Fire. What seems like the basement is actually the original first floor. When standing under the sidewalk you are standing on what used to be the ground level and the large stone wall is one side of the raised street. The sidewalk, with skylights, connects the top of the street wall to what was originally the second floor of the building.

[16]
Mutual Life Building, Elmer Fisher, Emil de Neuf, 1889, 1892

Another one of Henry Yesler's commissions. Elmer designed what was intended to be a seven story building but the work stalled after the basement and first story were built. By this time, Henry's wife Sarah had died and it seemed that he was slowly becoming senile. His nephew, James Lowman, had taken over his finances but while on a trip back East, Henry met his young second cousin, Minnie. They married in 1890 while he was 79 and she was 22. They took a trip to Alaska and Henry died shortly after they returned. There was a huge fight for the estate and by the time Lowman was ready to finish the project, Elmer had already left Seattle so it fell on Emil, who redesigned the top floors. This is why the upper floors look so different from lower bottom floors. This building originally had the bare rusticated sandstone that Yesler liked so much but it was smoothed out during the later construction.

This is another place that you can go down into the basement and see the street wall that was built to elevate the city. And you should do it before this mom and pop toy store is gone. Get yourself a pack of Beech-Nut gum or a board game or something.

[17]

Emerald City Building, 1902 (Starr-Boyd Building,
Elmer Fisher, 1889)

I only know two things about the Emerald City Building. It was built in 1902, and its South wall still has the North wall of the Starr-Boyd building attached to it, which is obvious once you know to look for it.

The Starr-Boyd building is one of my favorite Elmer Fisher buildings. There are old photos of it and it's definitely worth a google. Elmer designed the building for two different owners of the property and they both had different ideas of what the building should look like. It's also obvious which owner put the most money into it. But now all that remains of it is a wall stuck to another wall.

[18]
Feuer Building, Elmer Fisher, 1889 (Emil de Neuf, 1892)

Elmer designed this building in 1889, but it was not immediately built. It was completed by Emil de Neuf in 1892 and it appears, to me anyway, that he held to Elmer's original design. There's not a lot of information out there about this building, so here's a little about Emil-

In 1894, when the work dried up because of the Panic of '93, Emil went to work in Guatemala and took up photography. He came back in 1900 and served as Mayor of West Seattle. He designed a Carnegie Library for Everett, WA before relocating with his family to San Francisco, where he worked briefly as a draftsman for City's Architecture Department. He died after falling off the fourth floor of a construction project, but it was not determined if he was pushed, jumped or if it was an accident.

[19]
Yesler Hotel, Albert Wickersham, 1914

This building was designed by Albert Wickersham. It was built later and presumably made to blend in with the neighboring buildings. It was a flop house for many years and is currently the only hotel in Pioneer Square.

Despite living in Seattle for many years, Wickersham only designed a few buildings here- this one, possibly the one directly across the street, the Seattle Hardware building at First South and King Street, and one of my favorites, the Maynard Building.

[20]

Schwabacher Building, Elmer Fisher, 1889 (Emil de Neuf, 1892)

The Schwabachers were three German-Jewish brothers who fled Prussian persecution in their native Bavaria. They operated successful businesses in San Francisco and Portland, and in 1860 opened a business outfitting gold miners in Walla Walla, which was suddenly the most prosperous town in the Washington Territories. They came to Seattle in 1869 and opened the city's first wholesaler, and then built the city's first brick building in 1872. They had many buildings and businesses, including Schwabacher's Wharf, where the SS Portland landed with its 'Ton of Gold' that set off the Klondike Gold Rush and made them outfitters once again. As Mark Twain said, "During the gold rush it's a good time to be in the pick and shovel business."

This Schwabacher building is actually a large L-shaped building with one front on Yesler and a bigger one on First. Both of Elmer's facades were originally the same but a fire destroyed the First Avenue side and Emil was commissioned to redesign it, resulting in two very different facades. Elmer's Romanesque front on Yesler is typical of his work while Emil's Renaissance facade show's his very different aesthetic. He not only used a cream-colored brick and different ornamentation, but he also smoothed down the rusticated stone to make it more modern looking.

[21]

Bank of Commerce, Elmer Fisher, 1890

Elmer built this building, originally called the Yesler Building, at the same time as the Mutual Life Building, originally also called the Yesler Building, at the same time as the Pioneer Building, for Henry Yesler. Most of Yesler's buildings had exaggerated rustication on their stonework and while the Mutual Life and Schwabacher buildings were smoothed down eventually, this one remains. Yesler no doubt wanted the rough hewn buildings to remind people of Seattle's raw beginnings, and that his saw mill and cookhouse were vital to Seattle's success.

This building was originally meant to be five stories but construction stopped after three. The top floor has been attributed to Emil de Neuf.

[22]

Terry-Denny Building, Saunders & Houghton, 1889

Charles Saunders and Edwin Houghton only did a handful of buildings together, of which just three survive, including this one. They formed a partnership when they arrived in Seattle but after a couple of years they parted company and each went on to design many buildings on their own. This building was commissioned by city settlers Charles Terry and Arthur Denny and the upper floors housed the Northern Hotel, popular during the Klondike Gold Rush.

This building is easy to walk by without noticing, and like so many buildings in Pioneer Square, it's best appreciated from across the street.

[23]

Maynard Building, Albert Wickersham, 1892

Albert Wickersham didn't design many buildings in Seattle, but I've always thought this building was magnificent. I used to drive by this building on a Duck and credit Elmer Fisher with being the architect but that was only because back then I didn't know what I know now. This building was originally the Dexter Horton Bank

Building and the VP was Rolland Denny, who had the distinction of being the first whitey born in Seattle.

This building is best seen from in front of the Buttnick Building across the street and every time I look at it I think that this is only the left half of the original design. Why would the main entrance be put there on the far right unless they hoped to one day tear down the neighboring building and finish out the right half of the design?

[24]
Lowman and Hanford Building, Elmer Fisher, 1890

This is another of several buildings built for Lowman and Hanford that was used by many different businesses over the years. While it may not be one of Elmer's most notable buildings, it's a reminder of just how many buildings Elmer was responsible for and how many still remain. A local publication at the time ran an article titled, 'Fifty-Four Buildings Designed in 18 Months by One Man' in which they called Elmer an architect of the 'highest attainments in their profession' and also claimed that he was involved in the design of 'a great many more'. I've looked at many other architects of that time, and to put it all in perspective-

Henry H Richardson (Elmer's inspiration)-
54 buildings in 19 years

William Boone (Seattle's 2nd busiest architect)-
53 buildings in 22 years

Elmer Fisher- 54 buildings in 18 months

[25]
Delmar Building, Hermann Steinman, 1889

This is another building that I used to attribute to Elmer on my Duck tours but was actually designed by Hermann Steinman, a German immigrant who made a name for himself creating breweries in St Louis before moving to Seattle. This appears to be his only surviving structure.

[26]
Olympus Cafe, Conradin Breitung, 1897, 1905

The first floor was built in 1897 and housed an apparently fancy restaurant called the Olympus Cafe. It was designed by Conradin Breitung who would go on to design a shitload of Roman Catholic dioceses, including St Alphonsus in Ballard and what would become the Good Shepherd Center in Wallingford. The top floors were designed in 1905 by Heins & LaFarge from the East Coast, who were in town to work on St James Cathedral (see- Assistant to the Director of Vitality) on First Hill. They also designed Saint John the Divine in New York City, which is said to be the largest cathedral in the world, but that seems suspect to me.

[27]
Lippy Building, Edwin Houghton, 1901

After his partnership with Charles Saunders ended, Houghton designed the Moore Theater, which is spectacular, as well as a multitude of vaudeville theaters and opera houses all over the country, all much more impressive than this building.

[28]

The Buildings on the West Side of First Avenue South
Between Washington and Main, 1889

From the St Charles Hotel on Washington to the New England Hotel at First and Main, all seven of these buildings appear to have been built directly after the Fire, and all had retail space on the ground floor and hotel rooms on the upper floors. In growing cities like Seattle, during building booms and events like the Klondike Gold Rush, many if not most workers and even families lived in hotels rather than apartments.

The J&M Cafe was designed by Comstock & Troetsche, who also designed the impressive Grand Central Building across the street. The J&M Cafe is said to have hosted Jimi Hendrix, Curt Cobain, and Wyatt Earp, but they'll also tell you it's haunted so believe what you want. Next door is the Central Card Room, which along with the J&M and the Merchant Cafe, are the oldest bars in Pioneer Square.

[29]

New England Hotel, Elmer Fisher, 1889

While Elmer may have misrepresented himself, first in Victoria/Vancouver, then in Port Townsend and later in Seattle, he still designed and oversaw the construction of many buildings, both beautiful and solid. He presented himself to Seattle as a 48 year-old Scotsman with a degree in architecture and a history of many fantastic successes, when in reality he was a 37 year-old from Royalston, Massachessetts with no education who only started designing brick and stone buildings two years earlier.

And yet, of the buildings still standing in Pioneer Square, at least 12 are Elmer's, eclipsing even William Boone, who I credit with 6.

[30]

Bread of Life Mission, Bucheler and Hummel, 1890

This building has had many owners and businesses for the first fifty years of its existence, most notably Madame Matilda Winehill who operated a brothel here and whose name still adorns the building. The protruding bay was built out of wood as was popular before the Fire but forbidden in 1890, prompting a lawsuit. The brothel was okay, but the wood bay was a fire hazard.

Then the Christians took it over and turned it into the Bread of Life Mission, offering food, shelter, a shower and a bible for $2.

[31]

Grand Central, Comstock and Troetsche, 1889

Nelson Comstock and Carl Trotsche were business acquaintances of Judge Thomas Burke who invited them to Seattle from San Diego to open an architecture practice. They lasted for only two buildings, this one and the J&M Cafe, before breaking up the business and going their separate ways.

This is a wonderful building that was rehabilitated in the 1960s by Ralph Anderson, an influential architect who also helped preserve other buildings around Seattle, including the Pioneer Building. It was also the first home to Grand Central Bakery.

[32]

The Marshall-Walker Block, 1890, The Nord Hotel, 1890,
and The Quilt Building, 1905, William Boone

The Marshall-Walker Block is my favorite extant William Boone building and with all the rusticated sandstone it would be easy to assume it was one of Elmer's. Henry H Richardson's style of Romanesque Revival would fall out of fashion soon enough but Boone and Elmer thankfully celebrated it over and over in buildings that still stand in Pioneer Square. This is another building, which is also called the Globe Building or the Globe Hotel, that I would credit to Elmer Fisher on my Duck tours. Not out of any disrespect to Mr Boone, but more as a tribute to Elmer's propensity to lie about his past 'accomplishments'. This building was beloved by Seattleites as the home to the Elliott Bay Bookstore before it moved to Capitol Hill.

The Nord Building was built at the same time as the Globe Hotel and while not nearly as grand, it fit right in with the other hotels. The Seattle Quilt Building was the last building built by William Boone, who would have been about 75 at this time.

[33]

Frink Building, William Boone, 1891

The Frink Building started out as an iron works building, then it was a shoe manufacturer, and then a grocery warehouse. While most of the buildings on the North side of the Burnt District (as it was known at the time) were mostly nice office spaces and upscale hotels, down on this side it leaned more toward cheaper hotel rooms and warehouses. But these hotels and warehouses are still attractive and impressive, at least to me.

William Boone, like Elmer Fisher, didn't go to college to be an architect. And while Elmer just declared himself an architect, Boone spent 30 years from 1853, when he first got interested in building design, to 1883, when he opened his first practice, learning the trade under the tutelage of professional architects. He surely had to see right through Elmer's shit immediately and how could he not be incredulous when Elmer got major commissions like the Pioneer Building and the Burke Building?

Boone fostered many upcoming architects and served as the first president of the Seattle branch of the American Institute of Architects which passed a resolution stating that, 'only men of professional training shall be recognized as architects'. Whether that was meant as a snub towards Elmer isn't clear, but one of the first things Elmer did upon relocating to Los Angeles in 1904 was to join the Southern California Chapter of the American Institute of Architects, and was elected vice President the following year.

[34]
Cadillac Hotel, 1889

It's hard to say who should take credit for this building but it's probably not anybody you would recognize. What's more important is that it now houses the Klondike Gold Rush Historical Park, which is totally worth a visit. It's not so much a museum as it is a visitor's center for one of the smallest National Parks in the country. It's staffed by Park Rangers, it's free, and it's full of great photos and stories about the Gold Rush and how Seattle capitalized on it.

[35]
State Building, Elmer Fisher's Last Big Project, 1890

When the Schwabachers wanted a large warehouse with floors that would be capable of bearing 500 pounds per square foot, they again turned to Elmer. It took several months to design but was still completed in less than a year. I love the fact that, although it was meant as a warehouse, it, like so many other industrial buildings in this district, was still designed to be aesthetically pleasing. It shows a respect from the building owners, architects and city planners for Seattle's place as the Pacific Northwest's dominant city.

In just over 5 years, Elmer Fisher was responsible for about 75 buildings in Victoria/Vancouver, Port Townsend and Seattle, as well as a building each in Bellingham, Ellensburg, Yakima and Woodland, CA. And then, in 1891 after the State Building was completed, Elmer walked away from his practice. It could have been one thing that did it for him, but it could have just as easily been a combination of circumstances.

He financed or was partners in a number of the projects he was hired for, which probably seemed like a good idea at the time, but it also meant he was liable for a lot of property when the building boom stalled in 1891. And like with many creative big-thinkers, the business end of things is usually best left to a partner to handle. He was hit with several lawsuits in the beginning of 1891 and his reputation was trashed, which certainly wasn't good for business.

And when building did resume, more and more owners were looking for modern designs, less like the Romanesque Revival designs of H H Richardson, and more like the steel framed structures championed by Richardson's contemporary, Louis Sullivan. Although Romanesque Revival buildings can be visually stunning and make you want to just stare at them, they have their limitations. Materials like brick and stone can be prohibitive in availability and capability, but two of the biggest problems with these buildings, at least to the new building owner, are height and light. You can only build up about six or seven floors with stone and brick before the weight is too much for the foundation. And the walls of these old buildings are load bearing, meaning they have to be extra thick and don't allow for large windows, especially on the ground floor where the retail business are.

The newer steel frame buildings weren't limited in height and had 'curtain walls', non-load bearing walls outside the steel frame that allowed for larger and more efficient windows. Steel frame buildings could also go up much faster and cheaper than stone and brick buildings. And while Elmer didn't seem to have an interest in this new construction method, younger architects like his own Emil de Neuf did.

But there could certainly have been other reasons why Elmer quit his practice. In my mind, he had spent the last 18 months on a manic tear. And in my experience, bipolar manic episodes can last many months and they are always followed by a crash. I wouldn't be surprised at all if he took the slump in business and his financial troubles to take a breather and do a job that was without stress for a little while. In fact, it looks like he hung up his architectural practice, applied for a liquor license, and became the proprietor of the Abbott Hotel, which he had built and was a part owner in.

If slinging beer and whisky in a pioneer town was just what he needed for his mental health, it worked because soon he would run for local office as a Republican, back when they were still the Party of Lincoln and respectable. He was also involved in a company that supplied steam power to downtown businesses. And at about this time he met Charlotte 'Lottie' Willey.

Elmer and Lottie met while he was 41 and she was 23, although according to him he was 52, which is starting to get creepy, even for 1892. Although maybe not so creepy for Lottie as this was her second marriage, the first one happening when she was 14. Regardless, Elmer must have found enough peace to want to get married and have a family. He had two children with his first wife, Mahala, who he left in Massachusetts before heading West. And Lottie, a widow, had two children so he obviously felt now that he could take on some responsibility.

At about this time was when Elmer got hit with a $10,000 ($300,000 in today's money) Breach of Promise lawsuit, brought by Mary Smith of Victoria. Elmer and Mary met in Denver and lived there together for several years, as well as in Butte, Montana, and Victoria, BC while he started his architectural practice. After a couple successful years in Canada, he landed a commission in Port Townsend (the Catherine McCurdy Building), and before long he was setting up a practice in Seattle as well. It appears he told Mary to stay in Victoria and that he would send for her once he was established and making money, as there would surely be a lot of it.

Elmer apparently strung Mary along for several years, until she found out about his marriage to Lottie, which had been announced in the Seattle P-I. He was served with the lawsuit upon returning from their honeymoon in Portland, which had to be crushing to him because Mary was also being very public about how he had deserted her after they had lived together for many years as husband and wife. He was unable to get any architectural work and it doesn't look as though he was doing much of anything in this period. I can only assume he was in a pretty deep depression, and Lottie, in her eventual divorce papers would say of this time that he was "given over to idleness" and unable to provide.

So in 1894, after a failed attempt to restart his architectural practice in Seattle, Elmer abandoned his new wife and child and went to LA to restart his business there, no doubt promising to send money home to his family when he was successful again. And Los Angeles would be a perfect place to start because nobody gives a shit what you've done or what your reputation is in LA. His new city was booming and he no doubt thought he would be its premier architect in no time.

Elmer landed 8 or 9 commissions but they all appear to have been small, modest projects. I found two on google maps that remain, go to- West 17th St & Toberman St, Los Angeles in Google Maps and you'll see a yellow one and a green one next to it. There was an attempt to add a little ornamentation to the front but he was obviously taking anything he could get and these houses were certainly nothing to brag about.

Meanwhile, John Parkinson, who had started as a draftsman in Elmer's bustling office, had also given up on Seattle and relocated to Los Angeles to what must have seemed like the Next Big American City, ripe for huge, awe-inspiring constructions. Within a short time, Parkinson was building the first steel frame building in Los Angeles, then its first skyscraper, then its largest hotel. He would then go on to design many iconic buildings, like the LA Memorial Coliseum, the Grand Central Market, and the LA City Hall. John Parkinson would even bring his son into the business to become one of the city's most successful architectural firms.

In 1897, after three fruitless years in Los Angeles, Elmer gave up and found another way to make his fortune. He joined the tens of thousands of other brave and/or desperate men and women and headed North to the supposed gold fields of Alaska. He was up there for about three pointless years before resurfacing in Los Angeles. He came back with no money and seems to have spent a year or two as a carpenter before taking a job as office manager for the man who once worked for him, John Parkinson.

It would be easy to assume that this would be a dark time for Elmer. To have been so successful as the creator of so many beautiful buildings that would seemingly last forever, and then to spend the next decade failing at every turn had to have put him in a depression, most likely the deepest and longest he would ever had. It would also be his last. Most accounts have Elmer's death as having taken place in 1905 in LA, but nobody really knows for sure. There were no obituaries in LA, Seattle or Victoria, or even the slightest mention of his passing. I had always felt an affinity for Elmer (obviously) from the moment I first read about him. He was an untrained architect who lied about his pedigree, his experience and his age, but still he created so many incredible buildings, including the Finest Building West of Chicago. And within just a couple years he was all but forgotten, even while he was still alive.

I wanted to know everything I could about Elmer but there's only so much information out there. I thought it would be cool to get his death certificate so I ordered a copy from LA County for the year 1905 but there wasn't one. I had them try 1904 because John from the UW found an obscure reference date of December 8, 1903, but again, there was no record of his death in LA County. I was disappointed because I was sure he committed suicide and I wanted to be able to point to that as proof-positive that he was bipolar, which of course he was. But I also wanted everybody with bipolar disorder to take a little pride in his accomplishment- over 70 buildings in about 4 years could probably only be done while manic.

But then I felt a little guilty for hoping that Elmer died at his own hand. The depression and despair that make suicide seem like the only option are bad enough to wish on anybody, let alone somebody I genuinely admire. My disappointment and guilt lasted about two minutes, until I realized that I no longer wanted to know how Elmer died. I no longer care.

When my wife Vanessa and I divorced, she took our dog Chloe. The two of them lived for a while in a house with a nice retired couple for neighbors. Ellen and Tom loved Chloe and would dog sit her all day while Vanessa was at work. I helped her move out and we decided that Ellen and Tom would take Chloe on the condition that they never tell us when she dies, and they never did. I'm sure they're all dead now but there's something nice about not knowing for sure.

Maybe Elmer left town and died somewhere else. Maybe he took his life in a way that there would be no body, he was certainly clever enough. Or maybe he did make some money in the Klondike and when the time was right he changed his identity and lived a long, happy life. Now I hope I never find out.

When I first started researching Elmer, there was a Wikipedia page and some short mentions here and there, but not enough. It's not just because there aren't many people who have even heard of him, it's also because there wasn't much written in the first place. Fortunately, there's more information out there now.

Two great online resources are Alan Michelson's amazing PCAD, Pacific Coast Architecture Database, and the City of Seattle's list of preserved buildings. Alan is with the University of Washington, as is John LaMont, who may have found Elmer's actual death date, which has eluded everyone.

But the two greatest resources have been two books by Jeffrey Ochsner- Shaping Seattle Architecture (with other contributors), and Distant Corner: Seattle Architects and the Legacy of H. H. Richardson (with Dennis Andersen). Distant Corner is one of my top five books of all time. I got it because it has the most information on Elmer, but found myself constantly getting sidetracked until I had to just take a couple days and read the whole thing. I will always keep it handy for the perfect presentations of Richardson influenced PNW architecture and the spectacular old pictures of the buildings I've fallen in love with.

Visit online- pcad.lib.washington.edu and web6.seattle.gov
Books- Distant Corner, Ochsner and Andersen, UW Press
Shaping Seattle Architecture, Ochsner, UW Press

1
BATTERY
-SEATTLE-
SECOND
4
MARION
FIRST
2
3
BELL
-PORT TOWNSEND-
5
WALKER
JEFFERSON
9
WATER
QUINCY
11
6
10
TAYLOR
WASHINGTON
7
8
TYLER
PROSPECT
12
13
WEST HOLLY
-BELLINGHAM-
MORE
BUILDINGS
FISGARD
15
GOVERNMENT
WATER
ALEXANDER
-VICTORIA-
14
CARRALL
POWELL
JOHNSON
16
17
FORT
COOK
18
-VANCOUVER-

[1]

The Hull Building, Elmer Fisher, 1889

Alonzo Hull fought for the North in the Civil War and was an ardent Republican which, again, didn't mean the same thing then as it does now. I read somewhere that Elmer claimed to have fought in the Civil War but it's unclear how often he said that. Did he inflate his age to make it possible to have fought in the war or did he add eleven years to his age because it gave him more legitimacy as an established architect?

As the owner of a business, your first job is Lead Salesman. You have to build trust with each new client, and the more competence you can exhibit, the more money you can get. A lot of times it seems like a good sales pitch is the difference between making a profit and just breaking even, or worse. But it's never good enough to just talk a good game, you have to connect with the customer. Elmer had no problem doing that and that skill was as important as his talent as an architect. And for the record, Elmer was between 9 and 13 years old during the Civil War.

The Hull Building served many purposes over the years, but because of its location, it never seemed to live up to its potential. The upper floors were designed to be working class apartments but it would take over 100 years before people would appreciate them. Belltown was kind of a bust until the Dot Com Era made the neighborhood one of the most expensive in the city.

[2]
Austin A Bell Building, Elmer Fisher, 1889

William and Sarah Bell were two of the first pioneers to arrive in Seattle as members of the Denny Party. Arthur Denny, Carson Boren and William Bell claimed large swaths of land with little to no regard to the natives who were already using the land for foraging and seasonal lodging. They had become friendly with the locals, or at least that was how they saw it. Chief Seattle was the leader of the two local tribes and it's highly doubtful the Denny Party would have survived without his help in those early days. When the chief's wife died, Bell and Denny offered to make a casket for her that would presumably show the natives how to bury a person with dignity. They made the casket too small, of course, and had to remove some of the ceremonial blankets and cram her body in before they could bang the lid on. It was surely not the dignified burial they were promised, and after more indignities and broken promises, several local tribes joined forces and attacked the settlers in 1856's Battle of Seattle. William Bell was so unnerved by the attack and the possibility of more to come that he took his sickly wife and young children and relocated to Portland.

Bell stayed out of town for 14 years and in that time, the rest of the city grew and developed while his property, named Belltown, sat idle. William Bell died in 1887 and handed the property over to his son, Austin Americus Bell, who began developing multiple properties, including what would become the Austin Bell Building. Austin watched his father slowly die of a mental illness that could very well have been Alzheimer's. With his inheritance, Austin was now one of Seattle's richest residents, but by all accounts he was miserable. He had some fireworks go off in his face and he was constantly going back and forth to San Francisco for treatment to rebuild his lower jaw, which had to be extremely painful. And he saw the early signs of his father's mental illness in himself, so at only 35 years old, he killed himself.

His wife Eva and Elmer finished the building and named it the Austin A Bell Building. The upper floors originally had 65 office suites they couldn't lease and they were soon converted to apartments which also failed to gain tenants. The building was known as Bell's Folly because of all the money that was dumped into a building that was built so far from the city core. Like the Hull Building it would take over 100 years before they would finally be proven right and the building was filled with high income tenants.

The Austin A Bell Building was one of Elmer's first Seattle commissions and was built before the fire. Despite its location, it was an impressive example of what Elmer was capable of and it established him as a major player. It was eventually gutted and completely rebuilt inside, although the facade was mostly kept intact.

[3]

Barnes Building, William Boone, 1889

This building was originally built as an Odd Fellows Hall and like the Austin Bell building next to it, was built pre-Fire. This is the oldest building designed by William Boone that still stands and has been remarkably well preserved. This building went up at the same time as Elmer's Austin A Bell Building next door, which means this was possibly the first time William might have worked alongside Elmer. William Boone had been the main architect in Seattle for about six years and now this hyper, phony Scotsman was trying to take all the work? There's no way William Boone, a legitimate descendant of Daniel Boone, or so he said, would just roll over and be happy about. So he started the Washington State

Branch of the American Institute of Architects and made it so you had to prove you were actually trained by professionals, and not self-taught, before you could join. Still Elmer would put up about **five times** as many buildings in Seattle in that time period as Boone.

[4]

Burke Building Remains, Elmer Fisher, 1889

Washington Territory Supreme Court Judge Thomas Burke was one of Seattle's biggest boosters. He was crucial to bringing a railroad to Seattle and spent a lot of time traveling East to get much needed investment money. He owned several large buildings, but for the building that would bear his name, Burke asked Elmer to design him something resembling the chunky stone buildings going up in Chicago. He was particularly taken with the famous Rookery Building.

This building and the Pioneer Building were built concurrently and were regarded as not only Elmer's finest work but also two of the city's finest buildings. These two buildings cemented Elmer's place as Seattle's dominant architect and he actually got both commissions in 1888, before the Great Fire and only two years after first declaring himself an architect.

In 1971, the US Government bought up the entire block for their Federal Building and decided it was cheaper to put up something new than keep the Burke Building and incorporate it into something bigger, even though it happens all the time. As a consolation to the pissed off people of Seattle, they saved one of the archways and some of the terra-cotta work and sprinkled them around the site. The archway is at 2nd and Marion. If you are there, Google an image of the building to see what we're all missing.

PORT TOWNSEND

[5]
Jefferson County Courthouse, Willis Ritchie, 1892

While in Port Townsend, be sure to check out the aspirationally named Uptown. Port Townsend was so sure it would be the New York City of the Northwest that they felt the need to create a fancy neighborhood on the bluff that was close enough to be convenient yet too much of a climb for the drunken riffraff. They forged an agreement with the Union Pacific Railroad to join Port Townsend to Portland in the late 1880's in a pricey deal that was sure to bring with it unimaginable wealth. They set about building a smattering of Victorian style houses Uptown, a bunch of commercial buildings Downtown, a City Hall, and this huge County Courthouse. The Northbound rail from Portland was never even begun, while the Port Townsend's Southbound rail made it less than 40 miles before they came to a small mountain and couldn't figure out how to get around it. So Port Townsend never became the premier city they thought it would be, but almost everybody I know in Seattle loves to go to Port Townsend to get away from the hustle and bustle of a large city, especially now that Port Townsend finally has its very own brewpub.

So grab a couple beers to go and head Uptown to gawk at one of my absolute favorite buildings in Washington State, the Jefferson County Courthouse. This building looks like it should be Downtown Chicago, Boston or New York, but there you would never be able to step back and get a good look at it because of all the other buildings. It is as great an example of Richardsonian Romanesque Revival as you will see on the West Coast and you could probably fit all of the residents of Port Townsend in it at the same time.

Willis Ritchie grew up in Ohio and dropped out of high school. He enrolled in a correspondence school and opened his own architectural firm by the time he was 19. He landed a bunch of work in Kansas prior to moving to the Pacific Northwest at 25 years old. He opened an office in Seattle in 1889 and instead of focusing on commercial buildings for the reconstruction after the Fire, he submitted bids on all of the new county courthouses that were about to be built now that Washington Territory had become a state. He got the job to build the King County Courthouse in Seattle first and it was such an impressive structure it landed him this county courthouse in Port Townsend as well as the extant Olympia and Spokane courthouses. As talented as he was, Willis Ritchie made no friends among the other architects. Architect John Parkinson wrote an autobiography many years later and the only Seattle architect he talked about was Willis Ritchie and what a petulant little fucker he was. Architects were always competing against each other on projects but it seems Ritchie was not above a little backstabbing and conniving. His former draftsmen com-plained that he was always taking credit for their work and he was very difficult to work for. Still, the Jefferson County Courthouse is a fantastic building. The fact that it was designed by a 26 year old with correspondence school degree probably pissed off John Parkinson and William Boone more than anything. Like Elmer, he was also not invited to be a part of the Washington State American Institute of Architects.

[6]

Old Consulate Building, Elmer Fisher, 1889

Elmer didn't design that many fancy houses but two examples of his surviving Queen Anne style structures are this building and the Lowe-Hohenwarter House in California. Queen Annes or 'Painted Ladies' can be gaudy and overstated and it's hard to stay on this side of the line of outright garish, but Elmer managed to design two gorgeous Queen Anne style homes that are as tasteful as Queen Annes get. Both of these houses were designed by Elmer but he had nothing to do with their construction.

This one was built for Frank Hastings who was a senator and son to Port Townsend settlers Loren and Lucinda Hastings. Frank began construction of this high-end house on the speculation that Port Townsend was about to take off and he could sell it and make a killing. Instead, the economy tanked and Frank was forced to stop construction and eventually the partially built house went up for auction. It was bought by Owen and Mary Olsen, who finished the house and took in boarders to pay for it. One of those boarders was a German vice-consul who worked out of his bedroom, and the building itself was never an actual consulate. But the name German Consulate Inn sounded good so they went with that for a while.

It is now the Old Consulate Inn and everything about both the interior and the exterior is so perfect that it was named one of the Ten Favorite Hotels in the country by the New York Times in 2018. The fact that it is such a well-maintained inn means that it has been enjoyed by countless people over the years, which I'm sure would have made Elmer happy.

Palace Hotel, Pettygrove Building, Whiteway and Schroeder, 1889

William Whiteway and Julius Schroeder seemed to have formed a partnership specifically to build a bunch of buildings for the impending population boom in Port Townsend. Quite often, established architects would bring on a local partner to do the less glamorous tasks of running an architectural office. It seems William Whiteway, an established architect from Canada, brought on Schroeder, who grew up in Port Townsend, to help get more work. They were responsible for about ten buildings in Port Townsend in 1889, among them the Palace Hotel, originally known as the Capt Tibbals Building, and the State Bank Building, also known as the Pioneer Building, right next to it.

Whiteway and Schroeder really wanted the job to build the Jefferson County Courthouse, like many others who would be bold enough to bid on it. It was a huge project, about $3,000,000 in today's money and would have cemented them as Port Townsend's leading architectural practice. They submitted a proposal that they were sure would stay within the budget, but it came in second to Willis Ritchie's. Ritchie's proposal was not modest at all and when he was awarded the contract, William Whiteway flipped out and accused the County of corruption and attacked Ritchie's plans as unrealistic and sure to go over budget. The Commissioner fired back, that No, actually, the only reason Whiteway and Schroeder came in second was because they were local and he didn't want them to look bad in front of their neighbors. If he was gonna be honest about it, they would have come in fourth or fifth. Ouch.

The Palace Hotel is a gorgeous building and must have made for a very respectable brothel. A huge port city like the one Port Townsend wanted to be would need a proper Bad Part of Town and if you could keep all that ugliness in one place there would be no need for drunken sailors, thieves and 'Ladies just trying to make a living' to wander up the bluff to the Nice Part of Town.

The Pettygrove Building next door was built at the same time by Whiteway and Schroeder and housed a bank and hotel rooms. Both the bank and hotel failed immediately and the building was sold off as two separate properties and if you're looking for it, you can see that the two halves of the facade have been maintained a little differently over the years. This building, sometimes called the Pioneer Building, was built for Frank Pettygrove, one of the founders of Port Townsend. Whiteway and Schroeder built ten buildings in 1889 but nothing earlier, which is curious because Frank Pettygrove died in October 1887. I'm not gonna try to get to the bottom of that one. Either way, Frank Pettygrove was an important figure to what was then the Oregon Territory.

The building next to that, the Kuhn Building (architect unknown), was begun in 1892, by Judge Joe Kuhn, just a year before Port Townsend's economy came to a halt. They cobbled together the third and fourth floors and for a short time the building was the largest, most impressive hotel in town. But when it became obvious there was no need for such a huge hotel in such a small town, they dismantled the upper two floors and threw most of the bricks into the bay. Another great place to stop for a beer.

[8]

James & Hastings Building, Elmer Fisher, 1889

Loren and Lucinda Hastings were early settlers of Port Townsend and were among the first to make a bunch of money. After her husband died, Lucinda invested a substantial amount of money in a couple of commercial buildings, with the obvious hope of capitalizing on the coming economic boom.

The first building Elmer built in Port Townsend was for Catherine McCurdy, widow of Dr Sam McCurdy, the town's first physician. Catherine and Lucinda obviously knew each other and when Lucinda needed an architect for her first commercial building she called on Elmer. She shared the investment with Frank James, who ran the Customs House and several other money making ventures. Frank James did very well for himself.

Port Townsend in 1890 had about 4,500 people, compared to Seattle's 42,000. Without a railroad there would be no way for the city to flourish as a whole, but because of its large port, its remoteness, and the fact that it had the only Customs House on Puget Sound, several individuals were in a perfect situation to make a ton of money without having to answer to any outside authorities. Victoria, BC, for instance, was the largest processor of opium outside of China and the majority of it entered through the Customs House in Port Townsend. And although opium was still legal, the potential for corruption was too much for certain people to resist.

Port Townsend was very much a Wild West Town, but with a steady supply of ships. A huge problem (or opportunity, depending on your disposition) in Port Townsend was Crimping, or being Shanghaied. The Shipping Commissioner, Ed Sims, who was responsible for ensuring the safety of passing sailors, made a fortune working with Max Levy, the 'Crimper King', before going on to become a State Legislator. Max Levy had a full-on business supplying sailors to outbound ships, and if enough sailors couldn't be found he was more than happy to gather a couple drunken wretches instead. A crimper would often have a couple of assistants called runners who would get paid for each warm body they could find. One account mentions a runner who was trying to get his victim drunk enough to pass out so he could transport him to a waiting boat, but when he couldn't wait any longer he beat him unconscious with a barstool.

Max Levy ran both a boarding house and a bar for the sole purpose of crimping vulnerable men. Sailors in between boats would be encouraged to rack up a bill at the boarding house and bar and when they couldn't pay, Max would deliver them to a captain who would pay off the tab and give him a finders fee. By the time the journey was over the sailor would still be broke and the cycle would begin again. If you were a sailor passing through Port Townsend or even just an unwitting stranger there on the wrong day, you could expect to be shanghaied and dumped on a boat destined for the China Sea. There were only two groups of people that were safe from Max Levy- locals, because you don't want to take the nephew of a prominent citizen, and Native Americans, because they were under the protection of the Bureau of Indian Affairs and nobody wanted the Feds coming around asking questions.

This was all done openly and with little consequence, and Max Levy retired, finally, after TWENTY YEARS in the indentured servitude business and lived out his days in comfort in San Francisco. He had a couple scares from returning sailors who tried to kill him but the real reason he quit the business was because the maritime industry was modernizing away from sailing ships that needed lots of hands towards steamships that could operate with a much smaller, specialized crew.

[9]
McCurdy Block, Elmer Fisher, 1887

After a few buildings in British Columbia, Elmer decided to open an office in the growing United States city of Port Townsend in Washington Territory. He brought his friend George Clark with him and they formed a partnership, Fisher and Clark, but only built a couple buildings before George died suddenly in November of 1888 of a lung hemorrhage at 44.

Catherine McCurdy was the first person in the US to retain the services of Elmer H Fisher, International Architect. She settled on a large two story building with a storefront on the first floor and hotel rooms on the second. The design is similar to a couple establishments he was currently building in British Columbia, and it particularly looks like a pared down version of the Byrnes Building. Both buildings originally had chimneys ringing the edge of the roof so that each of the rooms could have their own fireplaces, but the chimneys on the McCurdy Building have since been removed.

Samuel and Catherine McCurdy were Irish immigrants who were among the first settlers in Port Townsend in 1854. They built what is said to have been the first building made of actual boards, not logs, and were determined to make Port Townsend into the next New York, the common desire among settlers of the Pacific Northwest. Samuel had a medical degree from Trinity College in Dublin which he put to use as a surgeon in what was called 'The Indian War', but was really more about the local native population fighting back to keep their land in a desperate attempt to keep from being wiped out. McCurdy helped establish the public school system, was the Federal Overseer of the Courts, served as Sheriff, and was co-founder of Port Townsend's first newspaper.

His biggest contribution to the Northwest has mostly gone unnoticed- he started something in Port Townsend called the Marine Hospital to deal with the multitude of mariners coming through the busy international port. The Marine Hospital was federally funded and was relocated to the, by now, much larger city of Seattle in 1933. It was yet another blow to Port Townsend who lost the Customs House to Seattle 20 years earlier. The new building was built on Beacon Hill by Carl Gould of Bebb and Gould, who were responsible for an incredible amount of Seattle landmarks, such as the Olympic Hotel, the Flatiron Times Building, Volunteer Park, the original Seattle Art Museum, most of the buildings at the University of Washington, and many more. The US Marine Hospital on Beacon Hill, now the Pacific Tower, is known as the first headquarters of Amazon.

[10]

Hastings Building, Elmer Fisher, 1889

Loren Hastings grew up in Vermont but dreamed of moving West. He headed out when he was 24, but got waylaid when he met his wife Lucinda in Illinois. After their first child was born (whom they named Oregon) they set off on the Oregon Trail bound for Oregon City which was in the Oregon Territory, back before Oregon was a state. Fun fact- people from Oregon do not pronounce Oregon with three syllables, it's pronounced with two, as in organ or Organ Hastings.

The Hastings settled in Portland for a few years, had a couple more kids and then, when the California Gold Rush hit, Loren headed down and made a small fortune selling picks and shovels to the '49ers. When he got back he became friends with Frank Pettygrove, who was one of the founders of Portland. The other founder wanted to name this new city after his hometown of Boston, but Frank was from Portland, Maine so he insisted on Portland. They agreed to flip a coin, like gentlemen, and Frank won.

The 1849 California Gold Rush was so massive it drew people from all over the world as well as growing cities like San Francisco and Portland. San Francisco lost 75% of its male population and most of Portland's workforce also left to strike it rich. With nobody left to do the work, Frank Pettygrove gave up on Portland

and started selling off his holdings as he convinced his friend Loren Hastings to do the same. They hatched a plan to abandon this dying town of Portland and go form a real city on the inside of the Olympic Peninsula on Port Townsend Bay. It was 1851 and if they got up there quickly they could create the largest port on Puget Sound and the biggest city this side of Chicago. Frank sold off his last piece of land for a wagonload of leather and he and Loren bought a canoe. Their route would be two rivers, a long stretch over land, and a scenic 80 mile stretch on Puget Sound. The trip was so arduous that Loren would not subject his family to it, so he bought a bigger boat and made sure the very first white woman to step off it and onto Port Townsend soil was his wife, Lucinda.

By 1889, with Loren long since passed, Lucinda, her children and the rest of the city took the initiative to make a deal with a railroad to run a line between Port Townsend and Portland, which by now was a major city. It would become a colossal bust but, for a little while anyway, things were finally looking up for Port Townsend.

A huge County Courthouse, a Post Office and Customs House were being built on the bluff and the population was steadily increasing. It triggered a bit of a building boom that coincided with the rebuilding after the Great Fire in Seattle and you'll notice the bulk of the large buildings on Water Street have a '1889' or '1890' on them. So to add to the James & Hastings Building and the Old Consulate Building, the Hastings family enlisted Elmer Fisher yet again to build what would become the most noticeable building in Port Townsend, even though he was building over 50 buildings in Seattle at the same time.

The Hastings Building is a Victorian Italianate design that was popular in Seattle before being supplanted by all the Romanesque Revival buildings. This style was big in California and never really went out of fashion there. There are still a lot of Victorian houses in Port Townsend that were built during this short boom period but probably the biggest reason why they're still here is because there was never any need to tear them down to make room for progress. Seattle, however, hardly has any left.

The Hastings Building has been more unoccupied than occupied for its 130+ years, which is a shame because the interior layout is similar to some of Elmer's greatest buildings, like the Pioneer Building and the Hill Building just a few doors down. To get natural light into the middle of the building, Elmer would sometimes design an atrium with skylights that light up the entire interior. The upper floors would have catwalks and the rooms would have windows facing inward as well as outward, which provided a surprising amount of openness. This building is still owned by the Hastings family and they've recently announced a major renovation.

[11]
ND Hill Building, Elmer Fisher, 1889

Nathan Davis Hill is another example of somebody who did what needed to be done to make a pioneer town succeed. He was a farmer and a pharmacist and built this building in part to house the Port Townsend area's first drug store. He also got involved in saw mills, railroads, and banking, and ran an Indian agency and was Jefferson County Commissioner.

This building is one of my favorites for a couple of reasons. In Year Two of the Covid pandemic I came to Port Townsend for a few days to see if I could figure out how many buildings Elmer actually built here. I looked for a reasonable place to stay and found the Water Street Hotel, which was in a beautiful building at a great location. I saw a picture of it online and it reminded me of some of the buildings in Pioneer Square, so I booked it. Once I arrived and went up to my room I was immediately struck by how similar the building was to the Pioneer Building, with its atrium, skylights, banisters and interior windows. I soon discovered it was one of Elmer's buildings, of course, and when I sent a pic of the interior to my mom she commented that it reminded her of the Brown Thompson Building, in Hartford, CT, which I later learned had been built by Elmer's biggest influence, HH Richardson 12 years earlier in 1877. A few months later I would go Back East and see the Brown Thompson, now the Richardson Building, myself and I can see why Elmer was so taken by Henry Hobson Richardson's work. Elmer surely saw pictures of the Brown Thompson building and I'm sure he was as mesmerized by it as I was and continue to be.

Another reason I really like the Water Street Hotel / ND Hill building is because it looks pretty much like it did back when it was built. This town was every bit as wild as any place in the West, and apart from the electric lights and upgraded plumbing, the building feels to me like it's still frozen in time. The rooms have high ceilings and period furniture and there's no better off-season deal than the Water Street. Or the Old Consulate. Or the Palace Hotel. They're all great.

BELLINGHAM

[12]
Lottie Roth Block, Elmer Fisher, 1890

This incredible building of Chuckanut Bay sandstone was built for Charles Roth, co-owner of the Bellingham Bay Quarry and named for his wife Lottie, who happened to be the daughter of the guy who founded the quarry. This was the rusticated sandstone Elmer used almost exclusively and at the time, Chuckanut sandstone was all over Seattle. Charles Roth wanted to celebrate that fact with a building of his own in what was then Whatcom County but is now Bellingham. When it was first built, the Lottie Roth Building was the premier office building with a bank on the ground floor. There was an atrium and skylights and exquisite woodwork throughout. But the commercial core moved to the East and the Lottie Roth Building was turned into a hotel and then apartments. Note that the two sides on the corner are beautiful rusticated sandstone and the other two sides are just brick. The building was never meant to be the stand-alone building it became. It was supposed to be surrounded by other large buildings. Still very cool, though.

[13]
Whatcom Museum, Alfred Lee, 1892

Just about six blocks away is the Whatcom Museum, built in 1892 as the Whatcom City Hall before Bellingham was a city. It was designed by Alfred Lee, a self-taught architect and mechanic who held a patent for a combustion engine, as his first commission. The construction, which includes Chuckanut Bay sandstone, of course, got off to a rocky start and it was never really utilized by the City. By the late 1930s the new City of Bellingham was formed to include Fairhaven and a newer, presumably better thought-out City Hall was built. Makes for a great museum, though.

VANCOUVER, BC

[14]

Byrnes Block, Elmer Fisher, 1886

Like many places on the Pacific Northwestern frontier, Vancouver owes its beginnings to the railroad industry, lumber and whisky. A man named Sue Moody began a lumber mill and in 1867 asked his friend Gassy Jack to open a saloon close by for the mill workers. The timing was right since Gassy Jack had just lost his beloved saloon, The Globe, when he left town for a couple days and entrusted the bar to his American friend who had a huge Fourth of July celebration and destroyed it with fireworks.

Gassy Jack offered free whisky to the mill workers who helped him build his new saloon, also called the Globe, and it was built in a day. The small town was called Gassy's Town initially, then Gastown. When the Canadian Pacific Railway was looking for its terminus, Gastown looked to be the obvious choice, on the condition they change the name to something nicer and since Canadians on the East Coast already knew of Vancouver Island, the growing city became Vancouver, and the original small neighborhood is still called Gastown.

George Byrnes was an Australian auctioneer who spent time in Victoria and then both mined for gold up North in Cariboo and served as Sheriff there. He bought some property in the developing Vancouver area, including a lot in the heart of Gastown that used to be Gassy Jack's second Globe Saloon, before it was destroyed in the Great Vancouver Fire. To build the first large commercial block in Vancouver, George Byrnes found Elmer Fisher, who was the very first 'architect' in the town to advertise his services in the local paper. This building was Elmer's first real commission and it was going to make a statement about both the legitimacy of this new town and Elmer's place in it.

The Byrnes Block is a large Victorian Italianate two story building that, when it was built, dominated this small town that was fortunate enough to be awarded a railroad. It was also considered the first 'fireproof' building in Vancouver. Elmer began designing it just after the Great Vancouver Fire of 1886, which broke out while they were clearing out land to build their city and prepare for the trans-continental railroad that any city would kill for.

The Byrnes Block has been wonderfully maintained throughout the years and still has all the individual chimneys for each of the high-end rooms of what was called the Hotel Alhambra. The chimneys are just for show now, as somebody realized having 40 fireplaces instead of central heating wasn't very fireproof. The building is right in the middle of the Gastown neighborhood and right next to the statue of Gassy Jack himself.

VICTORIA

[15]- Sheam and Lee Building, Elmer Fisher, 1888
[16]- Willes (Willie's) Bakery, Elmer Fisher, 1887
[17]- Cameron Building, Elmer Fisher, 1888

These three buildings are right in the heart of beautiful Victoria and don't stick out very much so you have to be looking for them. But these are some of Elmer's earliest commissions and this is where he taught himself how to be an architect. And how to be a 47 year old experienced Scottish architect instead of the 36 year old aspiring architect from Royalston, Massachusetts that he really was. Victoria and Vancouver are where he learned how to charm the clients so they felt comfortable with him, and then display enough knowledge and confidence to get the job but not so much that he came across as cocky or hard to work with. I've only found a few accounts about Elmer in British Columbia but they paint him as a very personable character and you can bet that if even one project went south, everybody would have heard about it and that would have been the end of that. But through intelligence and hard work Elmer learned the trade, developed a great reputation, and apart from the Older Experienced Scotsman thing, probably never needed to bullshit anybody too badly.

The Sheam & Lee Building is right near the Gate of Harmonious Interest, the welcome arch to the coolest Chinatown neighborhood in the Pacific Northwest. Definitely worth a visit.

The Cameron Building and the Willes Building, later called Willie's Bakery, are on the same block and have been very well-preserved. They are Victorian styled buildings that fit with the rest of the city and look nothing like the Romanesque Revival buildings he would later be known for.

The Willes Building was built for Louis Franz Willes specifically as a bakery. It had a 180 square foot brick oven that could bake over 300 loaves at a time and would often sell 1,000 loaves a day. It was Victoria's oldest bakery but changed hands a few times and finally closed 'for good' a few years ago.

[18]

Langley Buildings, Elmer Fisher, 1887

There are two wood Victorian houses right next to each other just a little East of Downtown that are examples of some of Elmer's first designs. They're off the same set of plans, pretty much, which is and was very common when building multiple houses next to each other. The detail is pretty amazing and intricate and thankfully both have been well-maintained. They were built for an AJ Langley and the Langley name traces back to not only Fort Langley but some of the very first settlers.

CALIFORNIA

Lowe-Hohenwarter House, Elmer Fisher, 1890

I saw this house listed in the back of Distant Corner but could never find anything else about it until I recently Googled it again. There's a website that posts daily pics of cool old houses with their dog in front (called- Walkies Through History) and in November of 2020 they featured the Lowe-Hohenwarter House. A Seattle acquaintance of Elmer's asked him to design a house that he wanted to build for his in-laws down in California. Elmer designed the building but had nothing to do with its construction since he had his hands full in Seattle, Port Townsend and Bellingham. And possibly Ellensburg. And a house in Yakima that was probably promised to Mary Smith. To see a couple pictures, Google- 'Lowe Hohenwarter House Woodland'.

Wallenslager Houses, Elmer Fisher, 1894

After Mary Smith came down from Victoria and sued him for breach of promise and Lottie Willey divorced him for being de-pressed, everything fell apart for Elmer in Seattle. And before he went to find his fortune mining for gold in the Klondike, Elmer spent a few years in Los Angeles trying to establish himself once again as an architect. He didn't get any of the big commissions he was used to getting and apart from a bakery, it looks like he designed only 7 or 8 buildings, mostly houses that he probably wasn't even involved in the construction of. He was living in a boarding room but that's all I know about his time in Los Angeles.

There are only two of his LA buildings I could find, but they're kind of depressing to look at. Google 'W 17th & Toberman St LA' and on the street view you'll see two of his last designs. At first they look nice and quaint with kind of a subdued Victorian style, if that's a thing, but also probably could have been sketched on a bar napkin. The fronts have some ornamentation but the sides are just clapboard and got no attention at all. Either Elmer had lost all interest by this point and was doing the bare minimum, or he was unable to get any good commissions and was reduced to quick designs for cheap customers. Whichever is most accurate, both are sad ways to end a career.

RELATIONSHIPS

I can only speak for myself and anybody who's ever been in a relationship with me, but being involved with somebody who is bipolar is probably more trouble than it is worth.

My wife left me because of my mental illness and no relationship since then has lasted very long. Relationships are hard enough as it is but adding serious depression followed by periods of manic behavior is too much for most sane people to handle. And it's not like being with somebody who is also bipolar is any kind of solution, that's only worse.

I have felt at times that I can pull off a long term relationship again but every time I try it's a failure. Every illness, malady or disorder comes with consequences, that's just how they work. With bipolar disorder you won't lose your hair because of chemo but you will go to concerts alone and you will get used to sitting by yourself when eating out.

Being in a relationship requires a level of selflessness that I don't think I have anymore. I can date and go away for a few days with somebody but that's the extent of it. Living with another person is not gonna happen again for me, I'm sure, but knowing that allowed me to build a tiny house to live in that is practical for just one person, me.

Finding companionship was easy for me when I was manic and unmedicated. And younger. It's no longer very important to me and I take it as it comes. If it is something that means a lot to you and you are bipolar then you will need to rethink that and come to terms with the fact that you will probably be alone more often than not.

So date, get laid when you can, jerk off when you can't, and enjoy those two week relationships because that's about as long as you get.

SHORT STORIES ON THE BUS

For my parent's fiftieth wedding anniversary, Mom and Dad and Suzi and Brent came out to Seattle to celebrate with a Duck ride. I chartered an entire Duck for them and my friends, and Ride the Ducks gave me 10% off because that was exactly how much they liked me. I spent about $800 and even allowed a Canadian couple to get on at the last minute 'cause this would be their only opportunity. They were made to buy tickets, even though I had paid for the whole Duck anyway, and were told they had to spend another $5 on quackers so they didn't miss out on all the quacking games.

The ticket sellers were pressured to sell as many quackers as possible because of the insane profit margin- Ride the Ducks bought them from China at about two cents each and sold them for $2.50. They came up with the brilliant idea to have an incentive program where the top seller of quackers every week would get an extra $20 in their paycheck. So I would see who sold the LEAST amount of quackers each week and give them $20. Cash money, no taxes taken out. Quacker sales dropped and management was pissed but everybody knew a Captain could do just about anything during the busy season and not get fired. Because it was so hard to hire and train Captains, we were irreplaceable. For about four months during the heavy tourist season, anyway.

A couple days after my parent's anniversary tour, the Canadian couple sent in an email complaining that they were pressured to buy quackers even though it was a private tour given by Captain

Braveliver who made it VERY clear there would be absolutely NO quacking onboard his Duck. Management took this as an opportunity to try to make me 'embrace the quacker' once and for all. So, of course, I handed in my resignation.

For the next two weeks I fantasized about what I would do on my last tour as a Duck Captain and I even wrote a short story about it and read it at a Ballard Writers Collective Annual Event. I dreamt of taking my Duck loaded with passengers through the Locks and seeing how far we could get. We'd aim for Hawaii but I'm sure we'd be forced to pull into Port Townsend for fuel and then all hell would break loose and that would be the end of that. I knew it would have gotten completely blown out of proportion and I know for a fact that my bipolar disorder would have been brought up by somebody somewhere.

I've always loved quitting a good job. It takes away any worries about getting fired and the Two Weeks Notice period is always very relaxing, mentally. It's like a cooling off period. And my last tours at Ride the Ducks were fun because I could finally talk about topics that were off limits and I didn't have to worry about swearing and pissing off the customers. Fuck 'em.

Every disgruntled Captain talked about what they were gonna do or say on their Last Tour but the reality was that management would schedule your last tour and then at the last minute send you home and make another Captain cover it. Captain Clem Chowder had to run my last tour.

Which was all fine. I was done being a Duck Captain and ready to move on to something else. I gave it some thought and decided on two career choices- a cop or a bus driver, as there were obvious benefits to both. If I was a cop I could fuck with my friends and I'd have an endless stream of crazy stories, but if I drove for Metro I could ride the bus for free. Both were excellent options and I decided that I would take the first one that was offered to me.

The police interview included a sit-down with two very experienced interrogators who wanted to be sure I wasn't a nut job, and a long questionnaire that probably took me an hour to fill out. One of the questions asked if I was on any medication for a mental disorder, and if so, what? I had to think long and hard on that one. If I said Yes, I probably wouldn't get the job because bipolar disorder has a bad reputation and the only reason to take lithium is if you're crazy. So I decided I would say No and then go off my medication just in case they actually test for lithium.

I said the same thing at the bus interview and wondered how many cops and bus drivers there are out there that have gone off their medications because they were afraid of being found out as having a mental condition? I surely couldn't have been the first.

It was King County Metro who offered me a job first, as a Bus Operator, but their training didn't start until February. The Seattle Police Department rejected my application without explanation, so I hunkered down and waited for the bus job to start. I don't remember anything about those few dark months but I know it was a low period. I don't do well with being idle and things would have gotten worse if I didn't have the bus job waiting for me.

I jumped right into being an Operator but first I had a month of training and a couple weeks of upgrading my CDL. I started looking for other jobs that required a Class B CDL but it was more out of curiosity than a real desire to switch jobs before I even started driving a Metro bus. The truth is, though, that I like applying for and getting jobs more than I like doing them.

The training was fun but when you actually start working for Metro you are constantly reminded that you're a worthless piece of shit. They bring you in as a part-timer and give you no indication when you'll be allowed to become a full-timer and it's best just not to ask, you filthy maggot. Full-timers won't even talk to you because you are somehow a threat to their way of life, although they won't tell you how. Part-timers are given 2.5 hours a day, Monday thru Friday. That's 12.5 hours a week to drive either the morning or afternoon rush hour shift. If you weren't happy with that schedule then you could do both the morning AND the night shift, you whining ingrate. Of course, you will have five or six hours of sitting around in between and NO you will not be paid for that. Maybe you just should have started your career with Metro twenty years ago!

Three times a year they have what they call a Pick. That's when all the operators get to choose their routes for the next several months. There are thousands of routes available and they're chosen strictly by seniority. Once the full-timers picked their shifts, we lowly part-timers were allowed to scrounge over the remains. I took the afternoon 64 route, from Cherry Hill, through Downtown and up to Lake City. The first stop was Swedish Hospital and on my very first day, a very cute woman with a shy smile and scrubs got on. Score! Nobody said there would be nurses!

The people who ride the rush hour buses were mostly down-town professionals who lived in the outlying neighborhoods and actually appreciate how efficient and affordable our bus system is. They say Hello and ask you how you are when they get on and always say Thank You and wave when they get off. And nurses! I was gonna love this job!

She wasn't there the next day and then it was the weekend, but she was there on Monday. She sat a little closer to the front this time and I imagined her staring at me, wondering what led up to me driving a 60' articulated bus for the largest metropolitan area in the Pacific Northwest in the coolest city in the United States. The stories I must have!

My route went up Fourth Avenue for a few stops before getting on the highway to go North. As I crossed Pike Street I could see that Ride the Ducks had their kiosk running for their Westlake Center tours. The Ducks ran their main tours year-round out of the Ticket

Booth by the Space Needle at Seattle Center but for their Holiday Tours and for the tourist season they ran additional tours out of Westlake Center in Downtown. The Westlake tours were exactly the same as the main tour, they just started in a different place in the loop.

Traffic was backed up and I got stuck at the light at Pine and Fourth for an extra cycle. I looked to see if there were any Duck captains hanging around and saw Captain Rick O'Shea. He was helping board passengers and chatting them up as they got on because that's what you do when you want to get more tips. Some captains disappeared for each break between tours but a couple of us went out and worked the crowd.

I pulled up next to him and sprang the doors open. He didn't notice so I honked my horn. He jumped in but stayed at the door. He probably wanted to be able to talk loud enough for my passengers but still not let his passengers hear him swear. "Jay Jay! How the hell are you?" I looked in the mirror and could see the cute nurse looking forward. This might give us something to talk about as she gets off.

Rick O'Shea was the longest running captain and pushed hard for them to hire me when I first auditioned. "I'm great," I said. "You should think about driving for Met-" but he cut me off to address my passengers.

"Your driver's crazy! I'd get off right now if I were you! HAHA!! He wrote a book, what was that? The Irish Cookbook? HAHA!! Take a bunch of potatoes and garlic and onions and throw 'em in a crockpot for two days? Boy, that'll clear out the pipes, am I right? HAHA!! He's freakin' nuts. He once made a Jesus doll to sell to the Christians. HAHA!! Got any more of them Hungry Jesus dolls, Jay Jay? HAHA!!"

The older buses used to have a handle to open and close the doors but now it's a button. I pushed it and the door closed on him, trapping him like a fly. "Hey! Let me go!", half serious and half hamming it up. "I told you he's crazy! He's trying to kill me." I moved forward a couple feet and he screamed a little. I laughed and opened the door so he could get out and drove away. There's my opening to talk to the cute nurse, I thought.

I turned onto Olive and then onto I-5. The 64 is on the highway until 65th and Ravenna, then you start letting people off. As one woman was getting off she leaned in and whispered, "Have a good night, you crazy motherfucker!" These people were gonna love me! If something happens they will totally have my back.

As we got to Wedgwood I heard somebody ask me how I knew that guy Downtown. "Oh, we used to work together. I used to be a Duck Captain," I said, like driving a Duck or a 60' articulated bus was nothing. Something any asshole could do. Then I realized it was the cute nurse.

"Oh! I love the Ducks. I've gone twice. Did you have a goofy name?"

"No," I said. "I was Captain Bravelier."

"I'm Lisa," she said as she smiled and got off. I had to remember that. Lisa. Lisa Lisa Lisa Lisa. Lisa Bonet. Lisa Loeb. Lisa Presley. Lisa MARIE Presley. Lisa Hartman, Lisa Hartman. Mona Lisa. I wrote Lisa on a transfer ticket before I forgot it.

I wanted to ask her out but I didn't know what the rules were because they never went over that in training. I could ask my union rep when I got back 'cause they seemed to know everything. Or I could hand her a copy of my book, but that was always risky. It's really more of a guy's book. But at least I got her name. Lisa. Lisa Lisa Lisa Lisa.

Metro had a program called Poetry on the Buses, where they would plaster the insides of buses with poems from local writers. Which is great. If you're into poetry. I prefer short stories.

On the way home I stopped off at Staples and got a nice black metal tray and a ream of paper. I printed out a sign that said, SHORT STORIES ON THE BUS, and a smaller one that said, FREE! TAKE ONE! that I put on the tray. I printed out several copies of a couple stories that I thought Lisa might like and that didn't make me look like an idiot.

At the base the next day, before I left for the terminal, I hung my sign and set out the tray full of several copies each of two stories-one about my time at Utilikilts, a Seattle institution that I imagined Lisa would know about and would give us something to talk about, and a racy story about Huggy Jesus in case she was wondering what the hell that guy from the Ducks was yelling about. About the only thing I'm good at with women is weeding out the Christian ones, and this version of the story would certainly do that.

My terminal (a terminal is basically just the place the bus starts or finishes its route. I learned that in bus driver training) was just a little down the street from Lisa's hospital and I could watch for her coming out the side door. The only thing I knew about her was her first name and what door she left work from, but I was smitten. It's amazing what one shy smile can do to me.

She got on last and I ripped off my sunglasses so I could make eye contact, which I did just in time and she smiled at me. Pretty girls used to smile at me all the time but now that I'm older I wonder if inside they're just laughing at me. But I am wearing a uniform and women love a man in uniform. It means they have a job.

Now the question would be whether or not she picks up a story. The bus is full before we leave Downtown so there's no way to see her until she gets off. There were a few other people getting off at her stop and she was in the middle of them. She said, "Thanks" and waved when she got off, and in her hand was one of my stories.

That night I printed out a few more stories and went back and forth for a long time about whether or not I should bring her a copy of my book. "Here's a copy of a book I wrote, that I just happen to have here under my seat!" Would that be too forward? Should I inscribe it? 'To Lisa, so nice to 'meet cute' you!' Would THAT be too forward?

She wasn't at the stop the next day so I waited as long as I felt I could and then rolled away slowly, watching in case she ran out. Which was fine. I don't need to see her every night. A little space is good, it doesn't mean she didn't like my story. Maybe something happened. It IS a hospital. Things happen in there all the time, probably. I did my route and went back to the base.

At Ryerson Base they don't really have a break room so much as a whole second floor, and it's usually full of operators. You have the part-time operators, like me, who were told to show up at least thirty minutes before their start time to check in, even though they don't get paid for it. It's bullshit and the union wouldn't stand for it if we were full-time, but the union doesn't represent part-timers. And the full-timers sit around on the clock doing what's called 'working the boards'.

Working the boards means you're qualified to run every route that runs out of that base and can jump in if somebody calls in sick. It takes many years to be able to work the boards but when you do you can make over $100,000 a year with all the overtime. Six digits to sit around and maybe run a route or two all day. Or maybe not even run at all.

And what did I hear every time I walked through the second floor of Ryerson Base? All these operators bitching about how they're getting screwed by King County and how all the new part-timers are somehow taking food off their plate because there are either too many of them or not enough, depending on who's bitching at the moment.

I learned in training that if a customer paid what it really costs for the average bus ride across town it would be more like $12 than the $2.75 they actually charged. That means King County is subsidizing your bus ride, and that's great. I'm all about cheap or even free public transportation. But it was wearing on me to walk up to the second floor before my measly 2.5 hour workday and get the stink eye and be treated like I was toxic just because I was part-time. It was also Election Time for the Union, which meant people were trying to get votes for President, VP, and all that. There were signs and banners all over the second floor and candidates making the rounds like it was the Iowa Caucus.

Candidates would work the room asking people what their concerns were and tell them that that was exactly what THEIR concerns were and how they would be the best person to stand up to those assholes over at King County. I realized pretty quick that once somebody learned I was a part-timer and unable to vote they would just turn and walk away. So all I had to do when I saw one of them coming was say, "Part-timer", and it would save us both the hassle.

I don't normally eat lunch but I figured out the right combination of food and liquids to cover me for my shift so I could focus on driving a large vehicle full of innocent people for two hours without needing to go to the bathroom- a small iced tea and a breakfast sandwich. I love a good breakfast sandwich but that wasn't always easy to do so I got a box of frozen Jimmy Dean Egg, Cheese and Canadian Bacon on English Muffin breakfast sandwiches. It wasn't great, but I looked forward to it and felt like it would be my new routine.

I'm chronically early for everything. I like to show up early so I can relax a little, do the crossword or something and not feel rushed before I start work. That's just how I am. But this day, I thought I'd heat up my egg sandwich and instead of eating it in the kitchen I'd take it out to my bus and hang out there and set up my stories. Get ready for Lisa.

Inside the freezer I found an empty box where my last sandwich used to be and instead of freaking out, I grabbed my backpack and went downstairs to find out who I'm supposed to quit to.

There's always a union rep and either the Base Chief or their second-in-command on site. The administrative offices and dispatchers are in a section of the building that is secured with metal doors and bullet-proof glass. I had to give the Base Chief a reason why I was quitting after only just starting.

"They ate my sandwich."

"Who… ate your sandwich?"

I pointed upstairs with my arm fully extended. "The Union. They ate my sandwich! I can't drive on an empty stomach, it's not safe! I quit. Do you need two weeks? Looks like you have plenty of people upstairs that could use something to do!"

She looked like she got it immediately and excused herself. She came back a few minutes later and handed me a frozen dinner. "Can you eat this and run one last time for me?" I felt like if some union asshole ate her sandwich she would have snapped his neck.

I tossed the frozen enchiladas in the garbage because I wasn't hungry and there was no way I was gonna go up to the second floor with some food the Base Chief gave me. I set up my Short Stories On The Bus display and when it was time, headed up to see Lisa. I was a little early so I sat at the terminal and watched the side door to see if she came out.

She wasn't there when I pulled up to my terminal and I waited there with the door open until one of the passengers complained, but she never came. I drove off realizing that I just lost a job and a possible girlfriend because some asshole ate my fucking sandwich.

Back at the base I threw out all my stories and signs and cleared out my locker. I almost threw out my Metro jacket but realized it wasn't just a jacket, it was a free bus pass and I still use it today.

About two years later I was on the 40 heading downtown and Lisa got on in Fremont. She was talking and laughing into her phone and sat in the middle of the bus. I was in the back and just watched her, imagining her looking back and seeing me before she got off, but she never did.

CLAN CRAIG
Crest- A knight in full charge with a broken lance
Motto- I Have Good Hope

They used to say about the Craigs, 'They're not very bright, but they're optimistic!'

GET A JOB

Most of my bad periods have happened when I didn't have a job, and that's not a coincidence.

Having a job means you have to be somewhere at a certain time and unless you want to work with a hangover, it also means you can't drink too much the night before. Not having the responsibility of a steady job leaves too much free and unstructured time for manic depressives so it's important to always be employed and, if possible, to have a schedule that gets you up early.

A menial job is better than nothing but it's much better to go for a job that requires some kind of certification or license. When I went for the job to be a Duck Captain I had to not only perform improv in front of a hiring committee, but also obtain a captains license and a commercial drivers license. The stimulation of preparing for tests is very healthy mentally and passing those tests does wonders for your self-esteem. These types of jobs also come with a slight bit of importance and novelty. It's always nice to hear, 'Gee, I've never met a Bridge Tender (or Duck Captain or Monorail Driver) before!' Doesn't happen a lot but when it does it's a little reminder that I put in a some extra effort and it paid off.

But one of the most important reasons to have a job is because if you have a reliable source of income, your side projects (painting, bagpipe making, writing, compost toilet building, whatever) can be just for fun and not for making rent. A full time job that you don't take home with you, just punch in and punch out, that both provides a decent living and allows enough time to pursue other things solely for the fun of it, may be as good as a manic depressive could hope for.

SLAP AND TICKLE

I recently applied to work in a railyard because working on trains is something I've always thought would be fun. The ad said I would be driving shunters and moving hoppers (whatever that meant) and would be expected to run all hours of the night. It sounded like a blast and the best thing about a job is that once it gets boring, you can just quit and get another one, so I sent in my resume.

I got a call from a guy with the Union Pacific Railroad and he nicely told me that he would never hire me. 'Never?', I asked? 'Never', he assured me. But he seemed to want to talk to me anyway because he found my resume interesting in the 'I'd like to have a beer with this guy but there's no way I'm ever hiring him' kind of way. We talked a little about the stuff on my resume- Duck captain, bridge operator, city bus driver, bagpipe maker, bell keeper, founder of Scottish Buddhism, boat builder, assistant director of Vitality in a senior living facility…

He made me explain why I only worked for Metro for two months (it was actually one month training, one month driving) and I had to admit that it was because somebody from the union ate my sandwich, and I was beginning to see why he had reservations about hiring me. He explained that my resume was all over the place and nobody wants to hire somebody who's just gonna quit and take some other job just 'cause it sounds cool. Which is exactly what I've done since I started working for other people. I can write it off as another aspect of being bipolar but the fact is that I don't want to work a boring job for the rest of my life and I can't just assume I'll kill myself before I'm sixty like so many other manic depressives do.

I learned a long time ago that having my own business doesn't work. When things are going bad it can set off a depression, especially if I have the pressure of meeting payroll every week. But when things are going well it's a whole other set of problems. When I was manic I was capable of getting some pretty big boat jobs very easily. Sometimes potential customers would come to my shop to meet me and step into a hive of activity. I mostly liked making things so I usually had a couple guys making a mold for a swim platform or finishing up a custom hard top or some other cool project. There would be music blaring and a fridge full of beer and all kinds of things hanging on the walls or from the ceiling to look at. I had an area where I was developing my bagpipes and outside was Steven's double decker bus and usually an art car or motorcycle being restored.

Sometimes I would have to go to somebody's boat to look at a job, like the time I met Karl, the King of the Stem Cells. I showed up in my kilt and truck with 'Boat Fetish' on the side, as usual, but this time I brought Courtney, who I'd met a couple nights earlier in a bar in Fremont. At that time I was going out to meet cute, fun women almost nightly. But I went to Fremont one night to chill out to some live mellow music and have a couple beers. I was determined not to hit on anybody and didn't even look around. But I got up and went to the bathroom even though I didn't need to anyway, out of habit. You'd be surprised how many women find the kilt interesting and it's not always visible sitting on a barstool. Sometimes you have to do a walk-thru. Right after I sat back down, before I could even finish my sip of beer, Courtney appeared next to me and asked if she could join me.

Courtney was a law student at the University of Washington but from Houston. Her daddy was in oil and after a couple drinks she told me that she used to babysit for Jeffrey Skilling's kids. She told me he started hitting on her as soon as she turned eighteen and she kind of regretted not sleeping with him at least once 'cause he got so famous after the Enron scandal it would have been like fucking Mick Jagger or something. Courtney was gorgeous and smart and fun and had a curiosity about random strangers like I've never seen. We stopped at a 7/11 once and she ran in to get a pack of smokes and she came out talking to an old black guy and continued for a full twenty minutes. She got in my truck and told me his whole life story and all I could think was that if she were fifteen years older I would have begged her to marry me. I hope she became a lawyer, she would have made a great one. Another thing she would do is when we were out to eat or at a bar she would start talking like we had completely different lives in a way that other people could overhear us. I'd play along 'cause it seemed to make her happy.

When we met Karl he was also taken with her. He called me out to Bellevue to look at his speed boat that had gotten trashed. He had just gotten back from six months in the Netherlands and his lazy idiot son had trashed his condo and his boat. Fucking pizza boxes everywhere. But his son made him rich so Karl felt like he couldn't kick him out. When his son was born, Karl insisted on being there. The doctor asked Karl if he'd like to cut the umbilical cord and Karl said, "That's why I'm here" and pulled out his own scissors and container, squeezed the stem cells out and ran them back to his lab. At some point people started freaking out about collecting stem cells, so Karl/Scotty's cells became worth a fortune. There were probably all kinds of things going on with that father/son relationship.

Karl took us out to the end of his dock and showed his boat. He'd been getting calls from other residents who were furious 'cause his boat was making the whole place look like a freaking ghetto. His son had taken his buddies out but when they came in they didn't put the cover back on it and it filled up with rain water and eventually collapsed the expensive lift that was supposed to keep it up out of the water. The interior was trashed and would have to be gutted, the motors were waterlogged, and if his insurance guy came out he would probably total it. But Karl didn't want to total it- he wanted to teach his kid some kind of lesson, even though he rarely used it. "Can you fix it? I don't care what it costs. I've got more money than I know what to do with", he said, making sure Courtney was listening.

Now that business talk was over, he wanted to know about Courtney so I just shut my mouth and let them talk while I tried to figure out how to get this stupid 40' speedboat on the broken boatlift back to my shop. Courtney told Karl that I had hired her as a consultant to market Huggy Jesus. She acted surprised that he hadn't heard of my stuffed Jesus doll and gave me a playful whack on the arm and said, "See, this is why you need me!" She explained Huggy Jesus to him and he totally got it. As we were leaving he asked for her number in case he came up with any ideas on how to get Huggy Jesus on Oprah. "No", she said, "I'm thinking bigger than Oprah", and slid into the truck and sat beside me.

Karl showed up at my shop a week or two later when I asked him for some money. He brought in a black bag and he looked around to see if anyone else was there but it was just me and Steven, who was welding something on a motorcycle. I'm pretty sure he was looking for Courtney. I showed him what we'd been doing on his boat, which started with gutting it out. It was now pretty much a shell. I had also hired a mechanic to get his engines running because if they had to be replaced, we'd want to know now. I asked him if had been thinking what he wanted me to do with his boat and said he was thinking that he wanted something to take to the canals of Belgium and the Netherlands. I explained that I could build a Maine Lobster-style cabin with an Alaskan bulkhead on his Florida-style drug runner hull with rebuilt dual 450's, but it wasn't gonna be cheap.

I showed him up to my office, which also had no Courtney, and he made a bit of a show of reaching into his bag and pulling out a clear bag that was full of money. He threw it at my chest and said, "Here's thirty thousand dollars!" I had never had anybody literally throw thirty thousand dollars at me and I wasn't sure what to say other than, "Okay."

He reached back into his bag and pulled out another, smaller bag with $10,000 in it, which he also threw at my chest. "Okay, that's good for now", I said, starting to feel a little nervous. I told him this thing could end up going over a hundred thousand so he gave me an American Express card 'for the books'. "Do what you need to with the cash", he told me, but I never knew what he meant. I made a mental note to invite him back when Courtney was sure to be there, though.

I never got into coke and you could count all the vacations I've ever taken on one hand. I'm a Scottish Buddhist so I don't care much about material possessions 'cause they're just a pain in the ass when you have to move. I already had a vehicle and the secret loft with a mattress behind my office was perfect for living in. So forty thousand dollars in cash offered no temptation to do anything other than build a lobster boat with an Alaskan bulkhead on a speed boat hull. And maybe grow my business. And bagpipes. Lots and lots of bagpipes.

With a little bit of cash and a bunch of other big jobs going on, I was able to hire a full crew and even a full-time bookkeeper. I was getting all kinds of fiberglass fabrication jobs and repair work and on top of all that I was developing a new kind of bagpipe that nobody had ever done- a Great Highland bagpipe made of composite materials. I was taking out full page magazine ads and growing my

<u>boatfetish.com</u> website. And then I had the brilliant idea to offer a scheduled cleaning service.

Darcy was a bartender at Mulleady's and she was, shall we say, physically perfect from a wealthy male boat owner's point of view. So I hired her to come out to a customer's boat and let me take pictures of her vacuuming floors, washing down the deck and waxing the topsides. I came up with a whole choice of packages, including the Slap and Tickle, which, for $1,000/week, would provide the discerning yacht owner with two attractive boat cleaners to scrub down their boat and maybe get into a water fight or something. Anything extra would be between the ladies and the boat owner, I wouldn't have anything to do with that part of it. If I could get the ladies to work for tips I wouldn't have to put them on the payroll, which was already starting to get pretty big.

Between payroll, rent and liability insurance my monthly nut was about $30,000, which meant I needed to land $30,000 a month just to break even. I had no line of credit and no plan for growing my business smartly. All I had was an infectious manic energy that made people want to work for me and customers give me money to make cool things for their boats. I get off on figuring out how to make and fix things and I always got a little high when I landed a job and got a down payment just in time for payroll and was so confident in my abilities that I didn't feel too much stress. After spending all day running four or five large jobs, my guys would leave and I'd work on my composite bagpipes. It was still in the early stages of development but I had no doubt that I was gonna be the Les Paul of bagpipes. If I could make artistic looking Great Highland bagpipes that sounded better than a traditional bagpipe, I would rule the world and let Boat Fetish run itself.

One night I was working on building a mandrel for making carbon fiber chanters (the flute-like part at the bottom of the bagpipe that produces the notes) when it dawned on me just how big this was. If I could make a carbon fiber chanter that sounded crisper than a traditional one made of African blackwood that was also stronger and looks cool, it would transform the entire music industry. I would essentially put the old chanter makers out of business, which would be good for the planet 'cause African Blackwood is endangered anyway.

The Craig name would soon be the benchmark in modern bagpipes. The custom composite Great Highland bagpipes would be the most fun to make but each one would probably take a few months to build and I doubted I could get more than $40,000 for each one, at least in the beginning. The Craig chanter, though, could be made for only about twice the cost of a traditional wood one, provided I make about a dozen mandrels and make a bunch at the same time. I had read that there were probably somewhere around 100,000 active bagpipers out there and if each one bought even just one of my chanters, I would be King of Bagpipes within a year.

I had been doing a little research into my Scottish roots and while I had known the Craig clan was one of the smaller clans (which I had first learned simply by the relative dearth of mugs and key chains with the Craig crest on them at the gift tents of Scottish festivals), I had recently discovered that, unbelievably, the Clan Craig had no Chieftain, which is why it was not a major clan. And it turns out there's actually some dude called the King of Arms of Lord Lyon who decides which clans deserve their own Chieftain. I got his contact information and sent him a long detailed description of what I was doing and how I felt that I deserved to be the Chieftain of Clan Craig, especially since nobody else was fucking doing it.

Next I sent off an email to Michael Craig, who was the President of the local Craig clan. I saw him every year at the PNW Scottish Games and while he was a nice guy and all, he was certainly not Chieftain material. Still, I apologized for going over his head, just in case I might need his support. But I probably wasn't gonna get it anyway because I stopped paying the $20 a year membership dues they kept hitting me up for the second I walked into the Craig tent. Twenty bucks just because my last name's Craig!?! No goddamn way!!

I was completely off my medication but fully focused on making my chanters and bagpipes. I would get really wound up and not sleep for days at a time and once spent about a week straight writing a patent for my carbon fiber chanter. I got the best law firm in Seattle to make it airtight, which cost me $7,000. There's a copy on my website- pages and pages of a patent-protected detailed description on how to make something that absolutely nobody in this world has any interest in copying.

But every great manic episode is followed by an even greater depression. Without my constant attention, Boat Fetish sank fast and I stopped taking on any more work. I told my guys to start looking for other jobs because I was winding down the business, getting rid of the massive shop, and getting a much smaller one to just build bagpipes in. It took about a month to wrap up all the jobs and I told all my customers I was no longer in business. All except for Blake, the president of Nordstrom and my greatest customer ever. He knew I had shut down my business but also that I probably needed something to live on, so he always had an idea for the next project for his Hatteras, the Fast Break. The Nordstroms were tall ('fast break' being a basketball term) so I made new shower pans that dropped down four to six inches so they could stand up straight in the shower without having to crouch. That kept me and Byron, the last employee who didn't seem to want to leave, busy for a month. And the jobs kept coming, even though it seemed like Blake was just making them up to keep us busy.

What if we made a new swim platform that was a foot wider so a couple extra kids could hang out on it, he'd ask? And how about a moonroof on the bridge that retracts? He never asked how much something was going to cost, just if it was possible. He gave us all kinds of projects and then took the boat up to the Gulf Islands for a couple of weeks. When he got back he said that his wife had a hard time sleeping 'cause the water was lapping against the hard chine at the waterline. He asked me if I wanted to maybe soften how the water hits the hull, you know, with some foam and fiberglass? He knew we'd have to do a haul-out and it would take a couple months, easy, but he didn't care, two weeks vacation on the boat was enough. The family wasn't that into it anymore, anyway.

After reshaping his chine I told Blake that I really appreciated him and all the work he made up for me but I really wasn't into working on boats anymore. The real reason though, was because I needed to be rid of Byron. Byron was a nice guy but he wouldn't leave, even with no more jobs coming in. He wanted to settle out the business and help me with the bagpipes and as happy as I was that he believed in the bagpipes, I was starting to really figure it out and I needed to concentrate. I needed to blast Butthole Surfers and bagpipe music at full volume, but Byron thought that was contributing to my depression. He insisted on playing his Christian rock station which played the same six God-awful Jesus songs over and over again until I'd have to turn the radio off and he'd finally leave for the day.

Byron was a Born Again and didn't take my Scottish Buddhism seriously because he said it was a made-up religion. He told me in his annoying-as-hell Chicago accent that Jesus was inside me and that he was the one who could get Him out and then I would be happy and full of God's love like he was. Which is exactly what somebody in a deep depression does NOT need to hear. Looking back it seems like he wasn't trying to help me so much as exploit my vulnerable mental state in a way to convert me to his religion and be able to parade me into his church. Just another reason I hate religion.

My former shop had been where I also lived and now that I had downsized to a small shop in the Fenpro building in Ballard I needed somewhere to sleep. My shop was on the back side of the building and I stored a couple of vehicles for my friends, including Steven's double decker bus and his sister's small old camper. I did a couple odd jobs for my old partner Paul and it was enough to keep me alive, and I lived in the camper without anybody knowing it for many months. I didn't want to go back on medication and I didn't want to kill myself because, even in this low point, I wanted to be around to see the bagpipes take off. I was never going to give up on the bagpipes.

I was out doing a fiberglass repair on Lake Union for Paul when I got a call from Steven. He asked me if I'd come over to his company and run Production for him. The department was a mess and he thought I had exactly the personality to pull everybody together and get the place running again, and start making kilts in-house. Although I had absolutely no idea how to start up and run a kilt factory, my depression ended at that very moment and a full eight month manic period was just about to begin.

FIND RELIGION

After my wife left me, my business failed and I was homeless for a period of time that I mostly can't remember, I moved into a group house with a bunch of young people. It was in the Seattle neighborhood of Ballard and had previously been a Buddhist Zen Center. It probably saved my life.

This Zen Center had been abandoned, and apart from one last holdover living in the basement and a ton of Buddhist memorabilia randomly scattered throughout the house, it would be my clean slate. There were fruit trees in the back and a compost heap that I first assumed was a rat feeder. Sitting around at night with various hippies, miscreants and outcasts, I formed my own belief system and encouraged everybody else to find their own path apart from organized religion. My dis-organized religion would be Scottish Buddhism, which I would later realize was also a metaphor for manic depression.

But every religion has to start somewhere, as they say, and mine started there. And unlike every other religion out there, mine would be based on the cold hard fact that life is short and you are going to die. There is no happy ending and no Supreme Being that gives a shit about you. Come to terms with that reality and make the most of the time you have here, Mr Craig.

The three tenets of my new religion would be simple enough, but also a means for me to deal with my bipolar diagnosis-

Take Care of Yourself, Be Nice, and Have Fun.

Everybody's different and has different needs. To think other-wise leads to organized religion, which doesn't really help anybody. You need to find your own way and if you need a religion to get you there, that's fine, just make it one that you can truly and fully believe in.

LATER, BRITCHES

There's no drug out there that I could have been injected with that could have pulled me out of my depression as quickly as putting me in charge of making kilts for my buddy's kilt business. I would be in charge of dealing with the local sewing contractors who made his kilts, his vendors, and the in-house Quality Control. The most important thing, though, would be to set up a factory that would eventually be able to make all of the kilts ourselves. I started immediately.

A few years earlier, Steven had started selling his kilts at the Fremont Sunday Market and got national press immediately. My mother called me one day and said that they saw some hippie selling everyday work kilts at an outdoor market and that my Dad wanted one. Was there any way I might be able to track him down? "That's Steven", I said. "He just moved in next to me. He comes by every night and drinks my beer. I'll get him one. I think Steven's calling it a Utilikilt." I thought they were dumb, to be honest. Steven swore he was gonna get millions of men out of their pants and into skirts but I wasn't buying it. I didn't say this, but I was just glad I got one for my Dad before he went out of business.

A week before that a local TV station came by to film a piece about Sean and Huggy Jesus at my shop and I made sure they saw the bagpipes I was making. Now they wanted to come back and do a feature about my bagpipes, even though at this stage, there wasn't much to show off. I asked Steven if I could borrow a kilt for a couple hours and he said, 'No way, you have to buy into it. No posers.' Fine, I thought, I'll just buy one and return it for my money back when he wasn't there. But as soon as I wore it once I was hooked. My wife of ten years was not a fan of the kilt, which she called the 'last straw', and left me immediately. I kept the kilt and suddenly understood Utilikilt's new slogan- We Sell Freedom!

The first couple of weeks as the Production Manager at Utilikilts was one of the best times of my life. Steven took care of getting a bunch of different sewing machines and explained how they all worked. There were single needles, double needles, sergers, bar-tacks, and buttonholers. There were snappers and riveters and we made a huge table for cutting. All kinds of cutters and shears and fabric storage and thread and all kinds of things I couldn't wait to be an expert on. We set up a turntable and speakers and a fridge for the beer. After a day of factory set-up, we'd go to a bar for dinner and strategize about what we would do once Utilikilts was outfitting the world. We discussed forming a political party, Utilitarianism, and developed a platform. He had long talked about a traveling caravan of buses full of performers that would show up to random locations to entertain the masses and sell kilts. Steven was doing really well and he was happy. He bought a great house on Queen Anne and now his drinking buddy, whom his employees all liked and trusted, was helping grow his business. Good times.

The Utilikilts Christmas party was at Sunset Bowl so after work we all piled into the company minivans. It had been Utilikilts' best year, by far, so on top of all the beer, food, and bowling we could consume, Steven handed out bonuses. I told him I didn't want one 'cause I'd only been there for a couple weeks but he put it in my shirt pocket anyway. 'You're family now.'

After a fun night of bowling, we picked a couple designated drivers, piled back in the minivans and went back to Utilikilts for our cars or to catch our buses. But it was still early and I wanted a couple of Guinness so I asked who wanted to go to Conor Byrne for a drink. I expected a few people would want to go but Betty was the only one up for it. "Great! Let's go!", I said.

Steven called me over and said he wanted to make sure I knew how to lock the main building. As he pretended to show me how a key works, he told me, "Fuck her and you're out of the company."

"What? We're just-"

"Fuck her, and you are out of the company."

I was surprised that he would even suggest this but I knew he had had a little drama with some employees lately so I let it slide and went for a couple nightcaps with Betty.

Right off the bat I started working seven days a week. Steven forbade it because he didn't want me to get burned out and told me No Sundays. But there was a small TV with rabbit ears so I could have a football game on while I was organizing the leather cutting area or hanging some lights in the back. I just had to keep the lights in the front off and park my car a couple streets away in case Steven was checking up on me.

Steven's new house was perfect for a New Year's Eve party. A piano, big deck, and a hot tub on the second floor outside the master bedroom. He even had somebody fill the place with helium balloons. At some point, well after midnight, probably, Betty and I went up to the hot tub. When it was light out and the hot tub was starting to get cold, Steven came out and threw a couple towels at us and I realized the door to his bedroom had been open the whole time. He seemed pissed. I could have left with Betty but I thought I should clean the house and do the dishes like a good guest, even if it meant asking Steven for a ride back to Utilikilts so I could get in my car and pretend to go home. Maybe I could smooth things over.

I did the dishes and cleaned off the tables. There were helium balloons all over the floor now and even though I had a raging headache, I grabbed a sharp pointy knife and started to pop every one of them. There had to be a couple hundred of them and I was almost done when Steven came downstairs and yelled at me that I had to leave. He looked worse than I felt, but he still agreed to drive me to my car. We got into the minivan without a word and I waited for him to say something on the ride, but he didn't. "I did NOT sleep with Betty", I said, trying to break the ice.

He couldn't help but laugh a little and said, "Well I know you guys weren't sleeping!" That was the last time we talked for about four months. He might have been ready to kill me for my dis-obedience but he wasn't ready to fire me yet. So he hired Larry, somebody with a deep knowledge of the garment industry who, just as importantly, would be a go-between for Steven and me. I would now deal with Larry so instead of asking Steven questions I would ask Larry who would ask Steven who would tell Larry who would tell me. This actually worked surprisingly well and for a while Larry was a fatherly voice of reason. For a while. Like, four months.

The first person I hired in Production was Lam, who I found through a Vietnamese headhunter. Lam was a great guy and we became friends immediately. We were the same age but born into very different circumstances. When we were both twelve years old, I was making balsa and tissue paper gliders and he was fleeing Vietnam with his family in an overcrowded boat.

Over the next couple months, Lam and I brought in seven sewers, a cutter, and a snapper. We had to learn how to make each of the kilts- the Original, the Workman, the Mocker, the Survival, the Leather, and the Tuxedo. The plan was to keep the sewing contractors on to make a steady supply of the most common sizes, but our new factory would be able to bang out late orders, custom sizes and colors, and the Leathers and Tuxedos.

Steven had requested a custom hot red mini Original kilt and we suspected it was for his new girlfriend. I'd been learning how to sew a kilt because I thought it was something I should know, but now, with the help of Mau and Mae, I was able to make this custom kilt from start to finish. I brought it over to the main building where I presented it to Steven and Larry. They were both impressed and Steven seemed happy that I took the time to learn this, so much so that we started talking again, gradually, and we were even able to have a couple beers together.

When I left the boat business to start a kilt factory, I got rid of all my tools except for the things I might need in the factory. The only things I carried on me were a fabric tape measure and a thread clipper. Steven noticed I wasn't carrying a Leatherman so he gave me his. I tried to explain I didn't need to carry one anymore 'cause I had a tool room with my tools in it right here and I associated a Leatherman with working on a boat out at the end of a dock when you don't have your real tools handy, but he insisted I take it and carry it with me.

I was taking the bus now 'cause I gave my car to one of the sewers who had an hour and a half long bus ride with three transfers compared to my bus ride which was about thirty minutes with only one transfer. I had been pretty manic the whole time I had been doing this job and I was trying to develop my newly forming religion to help calm me down. Randomly giving my car away without thinking about the consequences seemed like a very Scottish Buddhist thing to do.

I realized on the bus that night that Scottish Buddhism was a metaphor for my Manic Depression. It would never be a religion 'cause I would have to be the leader and the last thing I would want is a bunch of religious people expecting me to tell them what to do. Scottish Buddhism would always be private, just for me. Giving things away randomly would now be a part of it because look what came of it- It was about 1:00 am and I was sitting on a bus with a belly full of Guinness and I was feeling peaceful. I was being responsible by not driving, as well as being around people I may not come across everyday, like the Native American who was holding a watermelon and staring at me. I guessed he was about my age but had kind of a leathery face so it was hard to tell for sure. I wondered what, if any, guiding principles he might have, and I wasn't being judgmental, having only just started to work on my own. I wasn't even done coming up with my Eleven Demandments yet. I was wondering what he thought about life and death when suddenly he snapped at me- "What the fuck you looking at white man?!?!??"

He stood up with his watermelon and I got up, too, but I continued to smile and be peaceful. I didn't want to say too much because I was at that point where I was beginning to see double and I was starting to slur a little. But I wanted him to know that he didn't need to keep saying that I stole his land and that we were brothers so I pulled out my new Leatherman and was about to give it to him in brotherhood and peace, but suddenly had a huge craving for watermelon. We negotiated a trade, the knife for the watermelon, and he was demanding all my money (he was now holding my knife) when I pulled the cord for a stop and told him I was gonna throw his ass out of the bus before he could figure that the Leatherman that Steven gave me didn't have a knife blade. Steven gave me his old broken one and unless this guy was gonna poke me with the Phillips head or try to cut my hair with the tiny scissors, he'd better get the fuck away from me. He got off at the next stop.

I brought the watermelon to work the next day and when I offered some to Steven and told him how I got it (Scottish Buddhist Demandment # 2- Do Not Lie), he stopped talking to me again. Which was fine because he was just about to take off on a month-long cross-country solo trip in the shittiest car in the Utilikilt fleet. He gets off on fixing broken-down cars and this was his idea of a fun adventure, breaking down out in the middle of nowhere.

Even without Steven around, the business ran as well as it ever had. It was the first thing he noticed when he got back. The first thing everybody else noticed was that he was now wearing a turban. We were all curious about it but not in the 'What's up with the turban?', kind of way, but more like 'What do you think he's gonna wear next?', kind of way. I imagine there's probably a story behind it, maybe involving birds pecking at his head while he's doing a valve job in the middle of the desert, but I never asked. That can be his private moment.

After he was back for a couple of weeks he started to take an interest in what I was doing and how I was doing it, and I immediately knew what was coming next. I asked him to please not fuck with my system because it was working great, but it was his company and he could do what he wanted with it so all I could do was show him how I'd been doing things. I was at my desk one Sunday morning, stewing about it, when I called him from my desk phone because I had given away my cell phone. 'I'm coming up. We need to talk', I said. 'You better bring beer', he told me.

Halfway through the twelve pack there was an altercation and I ended up on the ground. Scottish Buddhists start fights but they don't throw punches, so I could expect to get beaten up a lot now. We tried to work things out and he invited me out for sushi (I don't eat sushi) but instead I went back to my office and wrote up my resignation letter, which was very short. The best resignation letters are always the short ones.

I loved my job at Utilikilts and I was very good at it. But when Steven decided to get back involved with his business, I knew my job would change. He was possibly just trying to learn how Production was running in case I flaked out and he had to step in, but I was so offended he would think that, that I had to quit. Plus, he punched me in the face and almost spilled my beer.

He apologized for punching me but I've been manic many times before and gotten into what seemed like bar fights, but were really just me looking to get a good beating. Sometimes, when my brain is racing and won't slow down, I need a reset, and nothing works like a good punch to the face.

I had given two weeks notice (I almost always give two weeks notice) and Steven and I were getting along again, kind of like a divorcing couple who can see that the end is in sight. He asked me to stay for another week, and I agreed to since I was realizing that I was about to be both jobless and homeless because of an unrelated living situation and I could use that extra paycheck. I was broke because I'd spent all my money over the last eight months self-medicating in the bars with Irish stout.

A friend gave me an art space downtown that I was using to mount a Scottish Buddhist Uprising in my free time. It didn't have a bathroom but it was all I had so I discreetly moved in for the two months that remained of the Uprising. (See- 'Nobody Respects the Scottish Inquisition', the Scottish Buddhist Cookbook, Another Book of Mormon, Kenneth Craig Publishing Company, 2015).

It was a dark period for me and it lasted several years. I was often homeless but Denny and Claire let me crash at their place and Paul gave me work and helped me buy a boat to live on. Lori had a machine shop and I worked on Boeing parts for about a year. But it all felt like I was just existing, and barely at that. Until I answered an ad to be a Duck Captain (See- 'Ride the Duck', the Scottish Buddhist Cookbook, Another Book of Mormon, Kenneth Craig Publishing Company, 2015). I once again found a job I could get excited about.

LITHIUM

The only times I've had a major depression in the last ten years was when I'd gone off my lithium, and that's only been twice. I still get it occasionally but it's pretty mild and I recognize it for what it is and I always know it will pass.

I started taking lithium about ten years ago at the suggestion of Dr Katie. I never had much luck with medications, except for the heavy doses of antidepressants that got me out of the worst depression of my life. But even then, they were prescribed in a way that sent me manic and were followed up by a slew of other medications in what seemed like an experiment to see which ones would work.

Lithium, unlike powerful antidepressants and heavy antipsychotics, is a mood stabilizer that has a proven record of effectively balancing out mood swings without sending you over the edge or crushing your spirit.

Lithium is a natural element that has been USDA approved for treating bipolar disorder since 1970. It can take weeks before it starts to take effect and even then, it's not a dramatic change. You will have fewer depressive episodes but the ones you get will be pretty mild. You will also have decreased manic periods but you won't lose the creative energy that keeps people like us going. If anything, you will be able to focus better and get more done. And actually get some sleep.

The real way to see if a medication is working is to go off it. A couple years ago my local pharmacy got bought up by CVS and for a couple weeks I wasn't able to get my meds. I went up to my friends' house on Whidbey Island and had my doctor call in my prescription there but by the third week things had gotten bad. I was beyond mere depression and manic thoughts and into full-blown rapid cycling, which is the most dangerous phase of manic depression. I grabbed a couple beers, sat in the hot tub and queued up a few of my favorite songs to go out on. Before getting the razor blade that I saw in the tool closet, I called my friend Caitlyn to see if she could ground me. That mostly worked and when I thought of all the blood there would be in the hot tub and how Laura would probably want to replace the hot tub and what a pain in the ass that would be, I rode it out and it was the last reminder I would ever need to never, EVER go off my medication again.

FRANK BRAVELIVER

Being a Duck Captain was a brutal job if you don't like being the center of attention. I had spent most of my working life building and fixing fiberglass boats, which usually meant being around the same small group of people. And unless I was drunk, I've mostly been a pretty quiet guy. Absolutely NOT Ride the Ducks material. At all. They always tried to hire people with acting or stand-up comedy backgrounds, so it was mostly failed actors and wannabe comedians, which explains a lot if you've ever taken a Duck tour.

I had been cycling back and forth between depression and mania and I couldn't hold a job to save my life, so, in an effort to save that miserable life, I made it my mission to get this job and everything that came with it, namely a US Coast Guard 25-Ton Master License and Commercial Drivers License. I honestly felt that if I could pull this off then maybe I would stop thinking about killing myself all the time.

The hiring process was brutal. I barely made it through, surviving two improv sets and an all-out campaign to convince them I was an extrovert. It was the hardest fucking thing I've ever done in my life. Being a goofy tour guide was easy for most of the others in my class and it seemed like they actually LIKED making people sing along and clap their hands and do quacking games. But I turned off my dignity and powered through, earning my captain's stripes before just about everybody else.

I was allowed to create a character and told that as long as it was working and people liked it, I could keep doing it. So I became Captain Braveliver, a surly Scotsman who could totally use a drink right now. I worked on my tour day and night and although I would occasionally get a little grief because some customer got offended by something I said, I didn't care. Most of my guests were laughing, applauding and I could count on the immediate gratification of $200 to $300 in cash tips, on top of my regular pay, for a twelve hour day with five tours.

There's a federal safety law that prohibits employers from working commercial drivers more than sixty hours a week, otherwise they would have worked us until we dropped. There's also a law that you're supposed to pay overtime after forty hours but they didn't start doing that until after the Accident. But sixty hours plus all the time I spent after hours researching history and coming up with fun stories was perfect for keeping me out of depression. It was exhausting but I loved it. I'd spend the day showing off my beautiful city and people would tell me how great I was and hand me money. After work I'd go get dinner and drinks until last call, then get up and do it again. It was a perfect schedule for a manic depressive.

As the season started to wind down I could sense that I would be among the first to go. I got ready for a low period but was pretty sure it wouldn't be too bad. I would be back for the next season, I just had to find something until then. That's when the Tour Director announced that Ride the Ducks would be doing Holiday Tours! I was thrilled, even though they were lukewarm towards my involvement. They figured on needing ten captains and since only seven other captains wanted to do it, they said I could try out.

This was 2013 when the driver was also the tour guide. It was also before cameras were added. I figured all I had to do was follow their script and play their music in training and as soon as I got the green light and was running tours, I could do whatever I wanted.

Holiday Training would start in October and tours in November, so I started working on my real tour right away.

One of my favorite parts of working with the Ducks was the training. Getting paid to drive around with other captains to learn a new route or practice safety drills or train new hires was like a paid day off to hang out with your friends. And one of the trainers was Richard, our Safety Guy and occasional captain, who I became good friends with. He thought my regular tour was hilarious and sometimes would take my tour on some false pretense just because he was always looking for new jokes.

The training for the Holiday Tours was run by Thom, the Tour Director, and Richard. We'd go out in a couple Ducks and drive through downtown, practicing our Holiday Tours and being obnoxious. Somebody brought in a bowl of candy and we threw it at kids, yelling, "Happy Halloween, ya jerks!" Thom liked me well enough but he never thought my tour fit in with what Ride the Duck was selling. But he thought my idea would be fun and said I could do it until people complained, so I bought a Santa suit, a hemorrhoid pillow and started researching custom embroidered hats.

The Holiday Tours ran from Westlake Center on 4th Avenue. They were nighttime tours that didn't go into the water and only lasted 40 minutes. We were worried that people would be angry about that but it turns out people were more upset about how cold it was. The side curtains were old and so hard to see through that we had to keep them up the whole time so you could see what few Christmas lights there are in Seattle. It was billed as a Holiday Adventure with Wacky Captains Leading Christmas Sing-a-longs While Enjoying the Festive Lights, or something misleading like that.

On my first night with a real tour, I drove my Duck to the ticket kiosk and pulled over a block before I got there so I could put on my big Santa beard and hat. I was already in my full suit but I put my hemorrhoid pillow in my coat to make me look fatter. I blared Mariah Carrey's All I Want For Christmas Is You, which was also the closing song on my set list.

There was a mob of people and I could already feel the eyes of every kid on me. "SANTA!! SANTA!!", they all yelled. I turned off the music and lowered the stairs and the kids looked like they were about to rush me. I made it to the ticket kiosk and slammed the door behind me while these kids all tried to look inside, like they've never seen Santa Claus before.

My Duck was loaded up and I don't know why, but I wasn't expecting nearly so many children. My Holiday Tour was going to be more of an adult tour and these kids were gonna hate me. And their parents were gonna hate me. And their grandparents were gonna hate me even more. What was wrong with me?

There were still a bunch of kids between the kiosk and the Duck and as they crowded me, I got into character. I wasn't Santa Claus, I was Frank, Off-Duty Department Store Santa.

"Get out of my way! What do you want from me?!? How about nothing? You want nothing for Christmas?!?! Get out of my way, you rotten kids!!! I've had a long day!!" Every kid froze up and I could clearly hear Thom laughing.

I boarded the Duck and made my way to the front. "HO HO HO!!", I yelled. "HO HO HO!! MERRY CHRISTMAS!!" I spotted Richard up at the front. He wanted a front row seat. "HO HO HO!!" I got right in his face and he was already shaking with laughter, "OH WHAT FUN!!!!"

I stepped onto the driver's platform and looked at every single passenger. "Look," I said. "I'm not gonna keep this up the whole tour, okay? I'm not the real Santa Claus, kids. I'm just one of Santa's Helpers. Santa's still up North making toys." I took off my beard and my Santa hat and put on the new baseball hat I had made that said

United We Santa embroidered on it and a couple large pins I also had made that said Chicks Dig Santa and BFD Local 86.

"My name's Frank and I AM a member of the local Santa Union. United We Santa! Oops, I'm supposed to be facing North when I say that." I turned around and put my fist in the air, "UNITED WE SANTA!!"

"And remember, always look for this union button before you sit on Santa's lap, okay, kids?" I took out the hemorrhoid pillow and threw it on the seat. "The REAL Santa has a shiny red sleigh with heated seats and a GPS. And I get an old WWII amphibious landing vehicle with a bad starter.

"So, I'm gonna roll you around in this old sled and we're gonna go look at some Christmas lights and do some sing-alongs, sound good? I'll be playing some songs you may or may not have heard before, but just fake it. All you gotta do is move your lips. That's what I used to do when I was a kid. In church. Or you can just blast your quackers. How many quackers do we have on board here tonight? Let's hear 'em! And we'll be waving at people, spreading some Holiday Cheer and wishing people a Merry Christmas and Happy Hanukkah. And of course my favorite- BE NICE!

"And most importantly, for God's sake, keep your arms and legs inside the vehicle at all times, because if you have to ask Santa for a new right arm, that might be all you get. That's kind of a big one. GOT IT? Good, Let's do this." I sat down in the driver's seat, put on my microphone, started the Duck and pulled out into traffic.

"Oh My GOD, what a day. You have no idea how hard it is to be a Department Store Santa. Any other Santa Impersonators on board? Anybody here ever play the Fat Man? I hope you were in the Union!"

I played my first Christmas song, in case Thom was listening, but as soon I was out of earshot of the kiosk I cut it off. "Only nineteen more days, kids. You counting down the days? I know I am. Just nineteen more days until December 26th and I start my vacation! 'Tijuana, aqui vengo!' That means Tijuana, here I come! 'Mas cerveza, por favor! It'll be sweet! And it'll be a whole 364 days til next Christmas! Yay!! My favorite Time of the year!! That's right, I'm going to Mexico, where they probably never even heard of Christmas!"

I don't remember what the next song was but it was quite possibly an offensive Mexican parody song that would be off limits now. But this was 2013 and it was on the master playlist. It was a different time.

"I don't like to brag, but I'm top Santa over at Nordstrom. Rack. Been there eight years. Got my own changing room and every-thing. And I deserve it. You wouldn't believe what I gotta hear all day- 'Santa, can I have a purple pony?', or 'Santa can I have an iPhone?', or 'Santa, can I have world peace?' You know what I tell them? I look down into their hopeful young eyes and say, 'No. No you may not. Life is just one big disappointment after another, kid. Get used to it.'"

Next song was I Ain't Gettin' Nothin' For Christmas, by the Reducers. I let this song play through 'cause the Reducers were a bar band from New London, Connecticut, where I'm from.

"One of the first things they teach you in Santa School is to get a good pair of shin guards. And believe me, you need 'em! Just today, I see this kid in line, giving me the stink eye, and when it's his turn he comes up and kicks me in the shin as hard as he could yelling something about some Power Ranger I didn't give him last year! And I was like, 'HEY! That's it, kid! You and me are DONE! It's OVER! No more presents for you! EVER!'"

I could hear Richard laughing but other than that, silence. This was going to be both my first and last Holiday Tour, which sucked because this was kind of fun. Broad Street has a good sized hill at Second Avenue that was a quiet zone during our regular tour because during the Summer all the people living in the fancy condos have their windows open and they call in and complain if they hear anybody having fun. But it was a cold winter night, and that was a different matter altogether.

I could see I was going to sail through the light at Second and said, "Everybody ready to go for a sleigh ride? Here's a Holiday classic by the Ventures. They're a Pacific Northwest original! Pull up your blankets, you're about to get a blast of ice cold Pacific Northwest air! And if your eyes start to water and your nose starts to run, go ahead and wipe 'em on the blankets we provided you. That's what the people before you did!"

I dropped the windshield down and BOOM!, we went over the hill like we were on a roller coaster and even though the tires didn't actually leave the ground, probably, every single ass left their seat. All of the guests screamed and laughed and I blasted some music and suddenly it was a fun tour. We made our way along the waterfront and I tried to go slow because you'd be surprised how mad a family will get when they fork over $60 for a 40 minute tour and you come in at 35.

As I pulled into Pioneer Square I said, "This is Pioneer Square, The Scottish section of Seattle. This is where I live. It's called Little Scotland and it was designed by a Scotsman named Elmer Fisher. Aren't these buildings beautiful? You won't see any holiday decorations down here out of respect for Elmer. As you may know, Elmer was a Scottish Buddhist like me and we don't celebrate holidays, especially the Christian ones.

"I was raised by Christians," I'd go on, "but now I'm a Scottish Buddhist. Scottish Buddhists are what you'd call religious, but not spiritual. Do we have any other Scottish Buddhists on board here tonight? Anyone? No? That's weird. I'm not allowed to proselytize Scottish Buddhism anymore, but you're allowed to ask me about it. No? Nothing? Fine. Whatever. Here's some bagpipes, then." Here

I'd play 'Jigs & Reels' by the Wicked Tinkers all the way through so I could have a bit of a break.

Ryan and Thom had been surprised when I said I wanted to do the Holiday Tours. They knew I struggled with being a performer and assumed I didn't like it. Plus I could be a pain in the ass sometimes because I don't like being forced to do stupid shit. But as I explained to them, I thought the Holiday Tours would help me do a better job on my regular tour. I refused to do YMCA but I decided I had to do something interactive because most customers are expecting you to act like an idiot. I had argued from the start that we'd get more business if we had a more intelligent tour but that was a losing argument at Ride the Ducks. If I was gonna do something stupid it would have to be fun. So I tried rapping.

"Seattle has a big rap scene, but I'm sure you knew that. We have any rappers on board? No? Really? Well, I'm gonna make rappers out of all of you tonight! All you gotta do is yell the last word of each line in a rap song and you're a rap artist!" I pulled out a large cue card that had a list of words on it- 1.DARK! 2. PARK! 3. FEAR! 4. REINDEER!, etc, and handed it to the person closest to me and told her to make sure everyone could see it. "READY?!? Put your hats on sideways and slump down in your seats. Let's roll this joint, my homies!"

We were crawling up First Avenue so I turned the volume all the way up and played Christmas in Hollis, by Run-DMC. If people weren't gonna play along, I would just move onto the next bit and forget about it. But they didn't just sing along, they shouted along.

It was Christmas time in Hollis "QUEENS!!" And Mom's cookin' chicken and collard "GREENS!!" With rice and stuffing, macaroni and "CHEESE!!" And Santa put gifts under Christmas "TREES!!!"

People on the sidewalk stopped and stared at us which only encouraged us to be even louder and pump our fists in the air. When the song ended I probably could have done it again, but we were getting close to Nordstrom and I had one more thing to point out before the tour was over.

"Hey kids! Look over there! See inside there, in that mob of children? See that fat guy in the red suit? You know who that is?"

"SANTA!!!", the kids yelled.

"No! I told you, Santa's still up at the North Pole making toys! Pay attention! That's my friend Butch!" I honked my horn and yelled, "UNITED WE SANTA, BUTCH!!

"You know, nobody has ever asked me what *I* want for Christmas. Just **ONCE** I'd like some kid to ask **ME** what *I* want for Christmas. Does anybody care what *I* want? I just want people to be nice to each other. I know it's too much to ask for everybody to be nice year round, but can't we do a better job of being nice for even just this one month? THAT'S the true meaning of Christmas, right there, folks- BE NICE! Coincidentally, that's also very similar to the main belief of Scottish Buddhism, which is- Be Nice. Or I'll Bust You Up!"

I took a left onto Fifth and cued up some traditional Christmas song, I don't remember what. Seattle doesn't exactly go all out for Christmas but there's a three or four block stretch where they fill the trees with Christmas lights. And since Ride the Ducks promised Christmas lights, we pretty much had to.

I could see in the mirror that people were smiling and all mellowed out so as I turned back onto Fourth I blasted Mariah Carrey's All I Want For Christmas Is You to take us back into Westlake Center.

The response to my Holiday Tour was exactly the same as my regular tour. People either loved it or hated it. Which was pretty much how I felt about running tours. Sometimes it was a blast and sometimes it was the worst job I ever had. But I didn't take the job because it would be easy. I needed a job that would force me out of the hole I let myself get into. When I applied for the job I was quiet and the owner couldn't understand why I didn't smile. Now I'm a lot more outgoing, confident, and even though I have to remind myself to do it, I smile a lot more.

And as I hoped, the Holiday Tour actually DID improve my regular tour. My second season was much easier and I was much more comfortable as a performer. I still refused to do any quacking games or sing-a-longs but I came up with something that was fun and interactive and that I never got tired of.

I still did the same intro, where I screamed till I was red in the face about how much I hated those goddamn quackers. It was funny but it also made it very clear that there would be no quacking on Captain Braveliver's tour. And I still rolled out of the parking lot with people clapping to the Go-Go's We Got The Beat.

But as soon as we hit the first light I'd kill the music and say, "So, I don't know if you know this, but we have a lot of Scottish people here in Seattle. In fact, we have more Scottish people here than anywhere else in the world. Well, except for Scotland. It's true!

"And as you know, we've got a big referendum coming up in Scotland. A big vote for independence! From the English! So if we see a Scottish person on the sidewalk we're all gonna yell 'FREE-DOM!!' as a show of support, are you with me?!?!" I would always wait a beat and somebody would always ask, "How do you know if somebody's Scottish?"

"That's easy. If they're wearing a plaid shirt then obviously they're Scottish. But another easy way to tell is if they have a bad haircut. See, Scottish people are… thrifty. We're… frugal. We're cheap. And we're not gonna pay TEN DOLLARS for a haircut when we can do a perfectly fine job ourselves!!" I removed my tam and pointed at my hair, which I always cut myself.

"So if you see somebody on the sidewalk and they have a bad haircut that means they're Scottish and we're all gonna yell,

'FREEDOM!!', got it?" It doesn't take long before you spot somebody in Seattle with a plaid shirt or a funny haircut. Or both.

It was perfect. We'd be driving down Broad Street and I'd say, "Oh my god, look at that kid, he's totally Scottish!", and the whole Duck would yell, "FREEDOM!!" And then on the waterfront I'd yell, "Hey, check out the haircut on that dude!" And everyone would yell, "FREEDOM!!", and the guy would smile and wave to us and everybody would bust up laughing. And, at least for a little while, I was allowed to do my tour the way I wanted.

On the first day of training at Ride the Ducks, Brian, the owner, came in to address the class and give us a lively pep talk and tell us we were ambassadors or some shit. Afterward he went over to Thom and asked him what was up with the guy with the beard. Why did I just stare at him and how come I didn't even crack a smile? Not even once? Thom told him that maybe he needed some new material but that he would work with me on smiling.

But in his pep talk he said one thing that I thought was stupid at the time but turned out to be completely true. He said that being a Duck Captain would make you a different person. And, really, how could it not?

RAPID CYCLING

Rapid cycling, at least as I understand it, is when your periods of depression and mania get so close together that they are no longer separate and you become manically depressed. It has all the energy of being manic but with all the negativity of depression. Your brain is going a hundred miles an hour and it's never anything good. Every bad thought you've ever had about how worthless you are drowns out everything. Your body is twitching and your hands shake and you're stuttering while you talk to yourself and you know how you must look so you try to avoid people.

This is when bad things happen. The whole reason I take lithium is to stay clear of rapid cycling. Mania is fun and depression sucks. But neither is particularly dangerous, at least in my case. When I'm manic I'm happy and I get shit done. When I'm depressed, I may hate my life but I don't have the mental energy to actually carry out killing myself.

Rapid cycling is when I've come the closest to suicide, but it's also when I've picked fights in bars, on buses or other random places. Usually it's when I've seen somebody doing something wrong, like making a woman uneasy or graffitiing something, and I feel like Batman, the only person to right this wrong. But really, I think it is often an attempt to get my ass kicked because I found that can be the only thing that brings me down.

Only lithium has minimized my journeys into rapid cycling and for that reason alone I will continue to take it for the rest of my life.

PUT ME IN COACH

The day after somebody ate my sandwich and I quit Metro, I contacted the people that operate the Emerald City Trolley. They did a City Tour that was a hop-on hop-off deal that was doomed from the start. The idea was that you could hop on at various points around the city, learn a little history from your tour guide, hop off at stops like Pioneer Square or Pike Place Market for a while, and hop back on to the next site. You could get a one or two day pass and ride around in what was billed as a trolley but actually an open-air bus. It would be the perfect way to experience Seattle!

They had already operated for a year and their TripAdvisor reviews were terrible. People would wait for two hours for a trolley to come around and when they did they were too full to let people on. There was a dedicated Helpline back at Dispatch but nobody ever picked it up because they didn't want to get yelled at. People demanded their money back constantly and took it out on the tour guides and drivers when told it would take three weeks to process. The hotels were pissed because they had told their guests they should use the Emerald City Trolley and when they did they came back and yelled at them.

To turn this ship around, Howard, the owner of the bus company that operated the trolley (not to mention the Space Needle, the Sheraton and a bunch of other Seattle institutions), decided to bring in the twenty year-old daughter of a friend of his. She had absolutely no experience other than teaching aerobics and working in a coffee shop. She supposedly had a year of college but wouldn't say for what.

Staci was eager for me to come down and sign up for the up-coming season. She knew exactly who I was and told me I gave a great tour. She had no doubt been looking on TripAdvisor and remembered the good Captain Braveliver reviews and disregarded the bad ones.

She told me that they wouldn't be starting the trolleys for a month or so but that MTR Western, the parent company, handled all the hiring and paperwork and wanted to get me onboard. They got me on the payroll and, because I now had a Class B CDL thanks to Metro, said I could start driving right away. Just needed a few days of training and I could drive these big, shiny luxury coaches until the trolleys started.

They had all the sports buses and moved professional and amateur sports teams around between stadiums and hotels. I imag-ined how cool it would be to pick up the Seahawks in one of the Seahawks buses at the airport and drive them home. I could invite them up to tell me about the game if they won and play some sad songs when they lost. It wasn't until later that I learned Coach Carroll requested the same driver every time because he knew not to say a word to anybody or even make eye contact. And, they didn't want the Seahawks buses anyway, just a couple nondescript ones. It was like driving around a bunch of nobodies.

On my first official day I was issued a black jacket and told I had to run down to the airport to pick up a bunch of people and then drop them off at the Red Lion in fucking Renton. I told them, sorry, but I have no idea where that is and I wasn't gonna learn on my first day with a bunch of paying customers on board. No way.

One of the dispatchers handed me a small piece of paper that said- R Forrest, L 6, L I-5 S, etc, like that shorthand 'map' solved everything. No way, I said. Somebody offered to print me a map but there was no way I was doing this. No way. Finally another dispatcher called over the driver who was originally scheduled to do this run and asked him if he could go along and tell me where to go. He was about to hit his limit on driving hours but could sit behind me and tell me which exits to take, if that would help. But I better get used to going to strange places with passengers 'cause that's part of this job, they told me.

Well, it wasn't part of the job with Metro or the Ducks. They would at least let you drive each route until you were comfortable with it. I was not feeling good about driving these things all of a sudden.

I was fine getting to the airport and had already been trained as to which parking lot to go to. And I learned something good to know about humans- they are mostly horrible people when they are separated from their luggage. Especially in that period between successfully getting their baggage from the airline and having to forfeit it all over again to the clown driving the bus. How can he do both jobs? Is he the bus driver trying to be a baggage handler or a baggage handler who's about to get behind the wheel of this giant bus? Most travelers aren't relaxed until they've checked into their hotel and all the luggage is accounted for and nothing was stolen from it. Next time you see a charter group getting on a bus at the airport, watch how many people will refuse to get on the bus until they have personally witnessed every single piece of their luggage be placed in the luggage compartment while questioning the bus driver who is, for some reason, doubling as a baggage handler.

I got behind the wheel and my fellow driver/guide-with-too-many-hours directed me out of the loading zone and out to the highway. I was completely unfamiliar with this area and I tend to stay off the highways whenever possible, anyway. The only vehicles I've had in the last twenty years were either motorcycles or crappy pickups and cars that could break down at any time. I decided right there that I would be the luxury coach driver that took the surface streets and stayed off the interstates. MTR Western would just have to live with it.

I could hear the other driver chatting up a woman sitting next to him so I assumed we had a ways to go before our next exit. Meanwhile I looked around to get a little more familiar with where all the controls were because we had Prevos and Hoolies and I tried to remember what the nickname for the Volvo was. I also tried to remember what that deal was with not letting it stay under a certain RPM for too long or carbon would build up in the catalytic converter or something, and it would stall and then you'd have to call in the mechanics to reset something and you'd look like an ass-hole and the mechanics would be pissed 'cause chances are they're home eating dinn- "THIS ONE THIS EXIT RIGHT HERE PULL OFF PULL OFF PULL OFF!!!", the other driver yelled as loud as an old fat guy with too many hours could yell.

We were about to pass the exit and I looked into the right side mirror as I cranked the wheel and saw the huge semi that was just barely behind us. The truck driver laid on the horn (like that was gonna do anything) and in an impressive bit of offensive driving, I placed that gigantic luxury coach between that semi and the crash barrels considerately placed just in front of the jersey barriers at the 167 exit of I-405.

I was shaken up, for sure, but I was not gonna think about it until I was back at the base where I would inform them that I would never drive a luxury coach again and they can go fuck themselves if they didn't like it. I almost got us on the national evening news for killing everybody onboard, including that other driver who was the only one who would have actually deserved it. To calm down I told myself I would go Mike's Chili and get a Monstrosity and drink beers until I had trouble walking home. And Amanda was working that night so that would help. I made my way back to the base thinking about chili, beer and beautiful Amanda.

I lasted exactly one day driving a luxury coach, which was fine with me and it seemed to be okay with them 'cause they told me to come back on Monday and I could start getting ready for the Emerald City Trolleys tours. Everything I've seen about the trolleys was pretty bad but it would be fun to be out there driving next to the Ducks, which to be honest, I was starting to miss a little.

The trolleys were always good for a laugh while driving a Duck, until we were told we had to stop mocking them. "Hey, everybody, look! It's the Emerald City Trolley! They're a hop-on hop-off tour and they just started a few weeks ago! You should check them out! Oh, and, look! It's their first customer! YAAY!", I said once when I noticed they only had one person onboard, which my passengers thought was pretty funny. I got called up to Tiffany's office after that and she asked me about something else that happened last week and wanted my side of it.

"Well, I was going down Broad St," I told her, "and traffic was backed up 'cause a train had just gone thru. I pulled alongside a trolley to say 'Hi' because they actually had a bunch of people on it. You know, just to be friendly and to show them how much more fun we were. But the driver didn't say 'Hi' back so I turned to his passengers who were sitting there looking miserable. I said, 'Hey, you guys alright back there?'

"So the driver totally fucking snubs me and turns back to his people and goes, 'Oh, don't mind him. He's just mad 'cause he has to wear a goofy hat. He'll go away.'

"Okay, so I'm wearing my Jimi Hendrix wig, which is white 'cause if Jimi was alive today he'd be 73 years old, right? And I yell, 'HEY! Here on the Ducks we don't HAVE to wear goofy hats, we GET to wear goofy hats 'cause here on the Ducks we like to have FUN! Right?!?' And all my people yelled, 'WOOOO!!', and I hit

Louie Louie on full blast and we drove away singing and boppin' around. That's all."

Trisha stifled a laugh and was smiling when she asked me to please not engage with the trolleys anymore because their manager keeps calling and asking us to stop, and I agreed.

And now I was about to be a trolley driver. The first day was an orientation and introduction to the trolley crew, including the drivers I had fun with last season.

Last year, Staci was a ticket-taker and was no doubt eyeing the position of manager. Now, Uncle Howard had given her the keys to the trolley operation and she had already been very busy. First was the swag- jackets, shirts, totes, caps, mini flashlights, and one Emerald City Trolley yoga mat that she would keep here in the conference room if anybody wanted to use it, just wipe it off when you're done.

First order of business was the chain of command. She handed out pieces of paper with five items ranked in order of importance. "If there is a problem, first go to number one." Number 1- Your Coworker, it said. "If you can't figure it out together, go to number two." Number 2- Dispatcher. I forget what number three was but Number 4 was The Police, and the last one was Number 5- Staci. "And NEVER call me on Saturday or Sunday. I only work Monday thru Friday. Take this and keep it with you at all times."

She made it clear that her job was not to micromanage us, but to make Emerald City Trolley the most popular tour company in the city. She'd already talked to all of the cruise ships about using us exclusively to drop people off at the downtown hotels and she had a couple other great ideas that she wasn't ready to talk about yet but we should still be very excited about, nonetheless.

Next she handed out the glossy little booklets that she had made up. "See all the advertisers? These booklets hardly cost us anything. And I already handed them out to all the hotels! Everybody take one and learn the route and when you need to be there. Memorize it." She looked at it proudly and held it up. "The 12 o'clock tour goes by the Sheraton at 1:05. Remember that. It's very important to go by the Sheraton at regular times. Howard gets a kick out of seeing the trolleys."

"An hour to get from the EMP to the Sheraton every time? How in the world do you figure that?", I asked, genuinely curious. Did she pick times out of a hat? "And this says we're going to Capitol Hill...?"

"It's a ninety minute tour with eighteen stops. That's five minutes between stops. Simple math."

The other drivers and I looked at each other and laughed. "That's not how traffic works," I said. "Can I make a suggestion?"

"No. I already made the booklets. You're too late." End of discussion, apparently.

"We've also been working on something you're all gonna love," she said. "We paid a LOT of money for this." A couple of the returning drivers knew what was coming and they just lowered their eyes.

"We're automating the tour. There's two voices, a woman's and a man's who do all the history and places to visit. They're hilarious. It's tied into the GPS so when you get close to the next landmark they automatically switch to the next talking point. And Starbucks gave us money so that's why we're going to their new Roastery on Capitol Hill. It's not a big deal. It's one stop, it'll take five minutes."

One of the tour guides raised his hand and Staci just stared at him until finally he asked, "Does this mean you don't need tour guides? I was counting on those tips."

"Everybody will love this new tour so much we'll ALL be getting tips. But your job will be to sell tickets. I'm going to train you all to take people's credit card information on these new phones. Drivers, too." She held up a phone and I didn't see a way to swipe a card and wondered if we would be expected to enter the card numbers manually. I would have asked but I thought I already knew the answer.

I looked around the room and realized that Malibu Staci never even bothered to have everybody introduce themselves. I recognized a couple people from out on the streets last season, like the guy who thought my Jimi Hendrix wig was goofy, and the Grey Poupon Lady, who, if you pulled up next to her and asked, 'Pardon me, do you have any Grey Poupon?', would pull out a jar of mustard.

My first thought was, of course, to quit. There's all kinds of driving and tour jobs out there and I could probably find something else before lunch. But I spontaneously quit my last two jobs and now I was about to quit this one thirty-five minutes into the orientation? This was not a sustainable career trajectory. I already decided I would never own my own business again so I would have to learn to stick out my jobs even if it meant doing things I didn't want to do.

"My name's Jay, by the way." It broke the ice and everybody started talking and introducing themselves to the few of us who hadn't already worked for the trolley. Staci got up and said she had to make some important phone calls and shut the door behind her, most likely not wanting to hear what we had to say.

I was looking forward to a couple weeks of paid training to drive the trolleys, which I knew would be fun and laid-back. Charlotte, the Grey Poupon Lady and I convinced everybody that the recorded tour wouldn't last a week and the tour guides would be giving their old tours again soon enough.

They didn't think things couldn't get worse than the previous year but once we started taking on customers things got much worse immediately. The recorded tour was abysmal and the customers kept asking for it to be turned off so the tour guides could do their own tour. There were a bunch of pre-paid ads that then didn't run and had to be paid back. The drivers and tour guides chose a new route and figured out a schedule that kind of worked but now the hotels all hated us because they were still getting yelled at by their customers all over again.

One of the managers at MTR Western sent out a group email about something and I noticed Howard's email in there. Howard, who owned the trolley, the bus company, the Space Needle, the Sheraton, a huge construction company, and I'm sure a bunch of other stuff. Getting his private email was a gift but I didn't want to squander it with a stupid, whiny complaint about just Staci. Having Howard's ear could be game-changing.

So I went to the Market Arms to think about it 'cause they had Fullers ESB, which is my thinking beer because it's so thick and rich and meditative. By the time I got home I was good and ready to fire off a long email about everything that was wrong with Emerald City Trolleys.

And since I'm a big believer in never bringing up a problem without also presenting a solution, I offered many. Namely, get rid of Staci. Just let us drivers and tour guides do our thing. But if you REALLY want to save some fucking money, why don't you sell all the trolleys except one and fill it with a bunch of actors and have it drive around your neighborhood and you guys can all wave at each other? Save the rest of us a bunch of hassle!

I wondered briefly if I should have waited until morning to send it but that's just something that people who aren't bipolar say. We had a Two Beer Policy at Utilikilts where no big decisions are made until you've had two beers. I lost count of the ESBs I had but I knew it was way more than two.

It was pretty late and I still wasn't getting a response from Howard. I figured I'd let him sit on it and respond in his own time but there was something that happened today and I thought it was pretty big, so I sent him a second email.

Earlier that day I was helping the tour guide board some passengers and one of them was very nice but older and was a little slow getting up the stairs. She apologized for holding people up as I took her arm, and her daughter exclaimed that she was ninety-two. Her daughter pulled out her card to pay for both of them but I insisted her mother wasn't paying. "Absolutely not! As far as I'm concerned, if you're ninety-two you shouldn't have to pay for anything!"

I had been thinking about that all day. Why should somebody who's contributed so much to society and made it to the age of 92 have to pay for fucking anything? It wasn't right. Senior Discounts are fine but this world needs FREE ATTENDANCE anywhere for people over 90! I suggested to Howard that we call it Esther's Reward in honor of her. What a thrill it would be for her! He needed to get the ball rolling and he can even take all the credit for it, I don't care. I don't need anything. He can start with the trolleys and the Space Needle, which would be easy 'cause I bet there's not too many 92 year olds who are gonna go up the Space Needle since you put in that new goddam glass floor, which I think was a huge mistake, by the way. I guarantee you your attendance will drop 80% because of that, so maybe this is a perfect time to start this. I assured him this would be HUGE and he didn't want the Eiffel Tower beating him to it, did he? And these 92 year olds aren't getting any fucking younger!

The next day was Sunday so there was nobody in the office but when I came in on Monday there was a note waiting for me to see Judd. My little manic period had passed and I knew what this was about so I took the Climb of Shame up the stairs and started thinking about my next job. I walked by Staci who was clearing out her desk and heard her say, "Well, you got what you wanted." What? For her to be fired or free stuff for old people?

I went into Judd's office and sat down. "I saw the email you sent Howard. Are you happy here, Jay?", he asked, like I've never heard that before. I assured him that, yeah, sure, I guess so. Never really thought about it.

"We're making a few changes around here. As you know, we've been getting a lot of complaints and we want to offer something to people instead of a refund. Howard said he went with you last week to pick up some friends of his getting off a cruise ship and you took them to Ballard and then down to see some fish or something. He said it was the best tour he's ever been on here in Seattle. He wants to know if you'd be willing to do your own tour of Ballard."

I stared off into space and thought about it for a little bit. Not whether or not I would do it, but how I would do it. I live in Ballard and know as much about the neighborhood as anybody. I also thought how this wasn't exactly a deterrent to sending off drunken manic emails at 3am.

"So I get my own vehicle, you guys give me customers and I can do the tour however I want and keep all the tips?"

"Sounds good," Judd said.

Yes it did.

PROJECTS

I don't think there is a correlation between being bipolar and being creative, at least from what I've seen. Everybody has creative ideas that seem interesting initially, but it's the manic energy of a bipolar person that brings life to even the stupidest of ideas. Tell a bipolar person their idea is crazy and their first thought is likely, 'Crazy? I'll show you crazy!'

I spent a couple of years and tens of thousands of dollars developing and marketing a stuffed Jesus doll called Huggy Jesus just because it was funny. I was eventually able to license the project to a pizza shop owner and I at least got all my money back, but more importantly, it gave me a way to channel my mental energy in a mostly positive way.

Next I spent many years developing composite Great Highland bagpipes. I got an X-ray of a traditional bagpipe and replicated every bore size and sound chamber out of brass tubing and fabricated the fittings to join them together. The patent I did for a carbon fiber chanter could be a case study in mania but it kept me busy in those dark hours and off the streets and out of the bars, for a while anyway. I built ten bagpipes that were absolute works of art, but only sold one. And that was for $500 'cause I needed money for food.

I wrote the Scottish Buddhist Cookbook one story at a time, with each story coming out late at night after beers. I automated a historic bell in Ballard while unable to sleep and built the off-grid tiny house I live in. I took up oil painting and did a couple pieces that people really liked but it never really grabbed hold of me so I quit.

I don't know what my next manic project will be (unless it's filling the world with Craiggers, my tankless composting toilet) but whatever it is, I know that it doesn't have to make me money in order to be a success. It just has to keep me engaged and off the street. Nobody has to appreciate what I do but me.

RING MY BELL

The Emerald City Trolley's website offered a 'Fantastic Ballard Tour with Jay', which got plenty of reservations, but it was also a means to placate pissed off trolley customers so they'd stop writing so many bad TripAdvisor reviews.

My tour started at the EMP turnaround between the Space Needle and the Ducks, so I got to interact with my Duck friends and then do two, maybe three, relaxed tours a day. And the best part was that if somebody was given a comped tour, that just meant they would tip me even better. I was making as much in tips as I was at the Ducks, with much less effort. I could talk about whatever I wanted to and was able to interact with people before we started the tour to find out what they were interested in. The website said we stopped at Gasworks Park, which is cool, and the Fremont Troll, which is cool if you haven't seen it a thousand times, but if people didn't care about those things, we just went straight to the Locks.

I knew one day that I had a couple who had scheduled a tour and it was looking like there wouldn't be anybody else coming along when they pulled up in an Uber. They were in their sixties but the guy looked like he was struggling a little to get in the bus. I helped him in and asked them where they were from and why they were in Seattle like I always do, forgetting that not everybody who visits Seattle is here on vacation.

She said that her husband was weak from some treatment and asked if we could just see some sights and not get out of the bus. Of course, I said, realizing that they were probably here while he was undergoing some kind of cancer therapy at Fred Hutch.

The night before I had gotten a text from Jake, who I knew casually from the Market Arms. He was a mate on the Northwestern, which was the star of The Deadliest Catch, and he said they were heading back and would be coming through the Locks the next day. I had told Jake a couple months earlier that if he thought of it to shoot me a text when they got back from salmon tendering 'cause it's always cool to see the Northwestern coming through the Locks.

I would guess about twenty percent of my passengers knew about the Deadliest Catch and only half of those have seen more than a couple episodes. I've never had cable so the only times I saw it was back in Connecticut when I watched a couple episodes with my Dad. Ballard is homeport to many of the boats on the show and Sig keeps the Northwestern at the Pacific Fishermen Shipyard which happens to be right next to the Market Arms.

I knew the Northwestern would be coming through but I didn't know when, so I kept my phone out, just in case. Before we even got to Fremont I got a text from Jake- 'approaching locks'.

Before I crossed over the Fremont Bridge and turned to go to Gasworks Park and the Troll, I asked my guests if they've heard of a TV show called The Deadliest Catch. The wife laughed, "Oh god, are you kidding me? He's obsessed with that show!"

"Really, well then I've got something to show you if you're up for getting out of the bus." I made a beeline for the Locks and explained that we probably weren't gonna see Sig, just so he knew.

"Do you think Edgar will be there?", he asked me. I had no idea.

I parked the bus and as soon as it was in park, Gary was standing at the door waiting for me to open it. His wife laughed and told him to let her help him. I got myself ready because I knew that as soon as the door opened Barbara and I would be racing to keep up with him.

I let Gary find the large lock by himself and as soon as he turned the corner he froze for a second before hightailing it over to the boat. Barbara was beaming and I thought briefly of sending Jake a text saying- 'guy in green shirt has cancer', but I didn't. Instead I told Barbara all about how the Locks work as we both kept one eye on Gary.

Gary spent the whole time with Edgar who was answering all of his questions and talking and laughing with him. And for the first time in three years, even for just fifteen minutes, Gary was free of cancer.

The Ballard Locks, also called the Government Locks or the Hiram Chittenden Locks, were built as part of an effort to connect Lake Washington to Puget Sound. It was first proposed in 1854 and that's when Lake Union was named because it would be the union between the fresh water of Lake Washington and salt water of Puget Sound. But after several failed attempts, the City of Seattle approached the Federal Government with the idea of making Lake Washington the Northwest Naval Base. The Feds went for it and paid for a canal and lock system so they could keep Navy ships in the fresh water of Lake Washington and go out into the salt water of the Pacific Ocean in times of conflict. And Seattle would get a fresh water port in the meantime.

After committing to the construction of a major waterway with a lock and drawbridges, somebody realized that the entire Northwest fleet could be immobilized if an enemy plane sunk just one ship in the canal or disabled the Locks. So the Federal Government moved the naval base to Bremerton, but was under obligation to not only finish the Lake Washington Ship Canal but to fund its ongoing operation. Which means that the Army Corp of Engineers pays for the operation of the Locks, and not only doesn't it cost the City of Seattle a penny, it also doesn't cost boaters anything to go through the Locks because it's a federal right of way. AND, the Locks are home to the Carl English Botanical Gardens, which is manned by volunteers, making the Ballard Locks both free to visit and free to the City of Seattle to operate. The Locks are my favorite place in Seattle and I got paid to show them off two or three times a day.

I would walk my tour group over the gates and watch a couple boats coming in or going out and I'd explain how the locks work. It still amazes me how they bring a two hundred ton fishing boat fifteen feet up from the salt water to the fresh water in just minutes, without using pumps. It would sometimes take a little while for people to get it, but once they did we could move on to the Fish Ladder.

If there was no other tour guide giving their presentation down in the observation area, I would jump up on a bench and give my presentation to both my group and the entire crowd, who happened to be lucky enough to be at the fish ladder when I told them all about Herschel the sea lion.

"...So we have mostly three kinds of salmon running through here now. The sockeye, or red salmon, come in first, in early Summer. Then it's the chinook, or king salmon, and after that, at the end of Summer, it's the coho, or silver salmon. There used to be another fish that came through here after that called a steelhead but they disappeared several years ago.

"Steelhead are an amazing fish. You've all heard of a rainbow trout, right? Well, If a rainbow trout stays in the fresh water it will stay the same size it's whole life, about five pounds. BUT, if you take that same fish and put it in the saltwater it turns into a steelhead and will grow to twenty pounds! It looks just like a salmon but it's actually a trout. Isn't that cool?

"Now, there used to be tens of thousands of these steelheads coming through here but now there aren't any. This whole run of steelhead got wiped out because of a sea lion named Herschel."

I could have told my group about Herschel outside but I found if I told it loud enough for everybody else in the observation area, some of them would run up to me afterwards and give me a tip. It's all about tips when you're a tour guide.

"A California sea lion started showing up when the steelhead were running and he kind of made a pig of himself. He would bite the head off of one and eat the belly of another and just kill hundreds of steelhead at a time! People thought it was cool to watch and somebody named him Herschel 'cause he looked like a friend of his. But the wildlife officials were starting to get worried that he was doing real harm to the steelhead run so they started doing things to scare him off. They started throwing firecrackers at him but he just got used to it and people thought it was mean. So then they installed underwater speakers that played orca calls but that didn't phase him at all.

"Then somebody had the brilliant idea to make a fiberglass killer whale to put in the water 'cause orcas eat sea lions. They named it Fake Willy and set it up by the entrance to the fish ladder. They went home all proud of themselves and came in the next morning and there's Herschel's sleeping on top of it! Pissed them right off! So they decided they had to get rid of him. They couldn't shoot him 'cause California sea lions are endangered but they had to do something or he was gonna wipe out all the steelhead.

"The only thing they could do was capture him and bring him as far away as they could. They brought him all the way down to Southern California and dropped him off at the beach and that was the end of that. About a week later they got back to the Locks, parked the truck, came out to the fish ladder and there's Herschel! Eating all the steelhead! And there's a bunch of other sea lions there with him! On his way back he met a bunch of sea lions and told them to 'Come up to Seattle, the steelhead are delicious!' And they completely wiped out the steelhead run and that's why there are no steelhead coming through the Ballard Locks anymore!"

People would thank me for including them in my tour and somebody would usually ask what happened to Herschel, which was great because it gave people time to dig into their wallets.

"Nobody really knows what happened to Herschel. He just disappeared one day. But some people think they brought him down to Florida. If that's true he's probably swimming through the Panama Canal right now! But really, what probably happened was they wiped out the steelhead and there was no more reason to come back here."

After the Locks I would take my group either for ice cream or down to Golden Gardens, depending on what they wanted. But I always took them to Ballard Avenue and explained how this was the best place to come for dinner, and if they were into live music this was the place for it.

I would casually drive up to the Bell Tower and park next to it and go over how Ballard used to be its own city, separate from Seattle. But after the Great Fire, Seattle built a spectacular water system while Ballard had an old system that couldn't keep up with its growing population. So Ballard was buying water from Seattle but eventually the Supreme Court said Seattle didn't have to sell Ballard water if they didn't want to, so they stopped and Ballard was forced to allow itself to be annexed by Seattle.

"And that bell up there, which was cast in 1891 to celebrate Ballard becoming a city, used to be part of the town hall and would ring when it was time to go to work, have lunch, go home and all that. But with the annexation there was no need for a town hall anymore, so eventually they tore it down and stored the bell over at the Locks. In the late seventies, some people got together and built this bell tower and put the historic Ballard bell in it. Which was cool but you rang it by pulling on a rope and some drunk broke it one night and it didn't ring for over twenty years! But then a couple years ago I automated it and since I'm the only one who knows how to ring and I'm the only one with the key, that means it's my bell, right? You wanna hear it ring?"

They always wanted to hear it ring, of course, and I never pass up an opportunity to ring it. It's impressed a couple of cute ladies I've met in bars, and one of the beauties of this is that if I'm ringing it at eleven o'clock at night because I'm drunk, there's nobody to complain to. Call 911 and they'll laugh at you and call the non-emergency number and they'll have no idea what to tell you.

The automation of the Ballard Bell happened about five years earlier and took only six months, start to finish. It was done by Peggy, Laura, Cass, the Ballard Historical Society and myself, but I still kind of consider it my bell. I asked Laura once if I could show her how to ring it in case something happened to me but she acted like I was about to kill myself and refused, like I wouldn't commit suicide if it meant there was nobody to ring it the next time the King of Norway pays a visit.

I had met Peggy a year or so earlier after she picked up a loose collection of stories I had on display at my friend's shop called Far Art and Beads. She had a column in a couple local papers and wrote a very nice review about them. Peggy met Laura at an event for a book Laura had done called Fishes and Dishes and they became friends immediately.

Peggy did a story about a beloved teacher in Ballard named Bertha Davis, who was 92 and in failing health. Peggy flat out asked her what she would like to see before she died and Bertha told her that if she had one last wish it would be to hear the Ballard Bell ring one more time. She had heard it regularly as a kid and was involved in building the new bell tower for it but it was never automated. Bertha told Peggy that 'a bell makes you feel alive!', and Peggy promised her the bell would ring again, even though she had no idea how. Until she remembered that Laura mentioned she was a member of the Ballard Historical Society.

A couple months later Peggy put together an evening of readings by Ballard authors that would become the Ballard Writers Collective. I was there with my just-self-published cookbook and seated next to Laura, whose last name is alphabetically close to mine. We all hit it off and within a couple days the three of us were plotting how to get the Ballard Bell to ring.

The Ballard Historical Society got a grant for $10,000 with no idea what it would end up costing because who knows how much it costs to automate an old bell? How often does it even happen?

I found a company to supply the striker and the electronics for $10,000 but that meant I had to design and fabricate an adapter and a box for the controller. And just as I was committing to a July 5th deadline for the official automation of the bell, my buddy Denny landed a job to build a bunch of metal birds for the airport in Juneau, Alaska and asked me to help. For about four months I worked on both projects with extremely little sleep but copious amounts of beer.

My day would usually start at nine or ten in the morning banging aluminum into ducks and geese and when Denny would go home I would go back to my boat and work out the details of automating the bell. I would work myself into a manic state which would be followed by a depression, and back and forth until I was rapid-cycling. I didn't sleep for days at a time and when I did it was only for a few hours. It was mentally and physically exhausting and those have always been the most dangerous times for me. That frantic state of being completely exhausted but not being able to sleep because you can't stop thinking about things for weeks on end is what I think about whenever I read about when somebody who's bipolar kills themself. Fortunately for me, I've got a bell I can ring the hell out of whenever I need to.

SUICIDE

The worst thing you can do when all you can think about is killing yourself is to not talk to somebody. If you're depressed and your life seems to be more effort than it's worth, find somebody to talk to and know that it will eventually pass.

But if you're prone to rapid-cycling you need to have one or two people you can call at any time. If you don't have that you need to have either a local suicide hotline in your contacts or now, just dial-

988

Many years ago my sister and parents made me swear I would never kill myself. So whenever I came close to doing it I would call one of them, and no matter what time of the night it was, they would have to talk to me.

I've only had to reach out to somebody a couple times in the last few years, both when I've gone off my meds, and I've spread it out among a couple of friends. Any family member or friend of yours will talk to you once they know how serious the moment is. And it usually doesn't even have to be a long phone call or visit. Just acknowledging it and talking to somebody who knows that you have worth is enough to get you through. And if you don't have somebody, there are trained professionals that will get you through that moment when nothing seems possible-

988

ASSISTANT TO THE DIRECTOR OF VITALITY

My Ballard Locks tours ended with the Summer and I had enough money to last me a couple weeks before I had to seriously start looking for a new job. I was working up my cookbook and wanted to do some kind of volunteer work or something, just as a distraction from writing.

I was at my bell one day offering to ring it for passers-by, when I noticed a bus full of older people drive by with the name Ballard Landmark on it. It reminded me there was the senior living facility just down the street where we had the party for Bertha as we launched the Ballard Bell automation project. Bertha was promised she'd hear the bell ring one last time, and she did. I met some really nice people there and I remember there was ice cream.

I went into the Landmark and was introduced to Gale, the Director of Vitality. I said I was just looking to volunteer to drive their residents around and give them tours of Seattle or something. Maybe one day a week, 'cause I have to finish my cookbook. I'm writing a religious cookbook with crockpot recipes, I told her.

We talked for a bit and really hit it off. She was a ball of energy and seemed to be really interested in letting me give tours. I would need to fill out some paperwork, of course, and it was starting to look like I wasn't being brought in to give the occasional tour, I was being hired.

The pay sucked but there was one free meal per shift and an open salad bar and I could walk to work and there was health insurance. And since I didn't have anything else lined up, I took it. I wasn't thrilled about it but I can always quit, I thought. Turns out she was having a hard time finding anybody competent who was willing to work for $16/hr. It was her lucky day.

I wasn't allowed to wear my kilt but I was kind of used to that by now. When I started training at the Ducks I was told I needed to buy some shorts 'cause apparently I was flashing my junk when I was inspecting the undersides of the Ducks while on a creeper. All the other driving jobs seem to have a dress code as well, and it was beginning to seem like the only employer who would ever let me wear a Utilikilt was Utilikilts. But when Gale handed me a god-awful purple polyester shirt with the word Vitality on it, I threatened to quit before I even started. I needed a pocket for my reading glasses and two pens, so it was a safety issue, I told her. It was kind of a big deal that everybody in the company wore different colored shirts according to their department. But I didn't ask for this job and I'm not going out in public, which is what drivers do, wearing a purple freaking shirt, I told her. I'll be wearing my green plaid shirts or I'll get back to working on my cookbook. There was a discussion with upper management but they relented and I got to keep my new job with shitty pay that I didn't want in the first place, wearing my green plaid shirts with a pocket for my glasses and pens.

My initial job was to bring residents to their doctor's appointments two days a week, and then one day I could do random tours of Seattle and whatever else I wanted. The doctor runs were hectic but you get to really know people when you're one-on-one with them in a car and they want to talk about anything else but their doctor visit. The tours were always full and I had to add a second one in the afternoon. I called them Mystery Tours to make them sound exciting but the truth was I often didn't have any idea where we would be going until the night before. Then I would choose a theme or a destination and do some quick research and print out some photos or something. One of the reasons I love Seattle is because there is no shortage of interesting things to see or learn about and it was fun to share it with people who couldn't wait to go on an outing. Especially Dorothy, who waited for the signup sheet to come out on Tuesdays and signed up for both the morning and afternoon tours, every time. When she died her daughter wrote in her obituary, "… and now Mom is on her very last Mystery Tour."

I started a WWII discussion group and made it clear that I wasn't so much interested in stories about fighting on the Front Line, I was more curious about what it was like to be on the Homefront. Part of that was the hard reality that there are no longer that many men who fought in WWII, and if they did, they were probably long past talking about it. But there was no shortage of ladies who could tell me all about rations, brothers who never came home, the bags of oleo with the yellow dye in them, propaganda posters, and the trainloads of scared young men who just finished their training who would stop in their town for one last dance before shipping off to war.

A few residents grew up in Norway and we learned about what it was like to be a kid living under Nazi occupation. Another had a father in the German army and told us about how she and her sister were smuggled out on a train at the end of the war. We heard about a time when, as a young boy, one resident watched as an American plane came in low to hit a building with Nazi soldiers on the ground floor and must have known the top floor was full of civilians, who all survived. People cheered, he told us, but the pilot lost control and slammed into a school building killing dozens of his classmates. As soon as he finished his story, he got up and left and never came back to the group.

If we talked about propaganda one week, I would research everything I could and print out a bunch of posters and explain what they meant. "Loose Lips Sink Ships", we learned, was meant to keep people from saying anything if they saw German U-boats off the East Coast because it would only freak people out and cause a panic. One resident worked for Boeing building B-17 bombers, an actual Rosie the Riveter. She didn't know it at the time but later learned that the building had actually been camouflaged. It was called Building Two and as we entered the war, there was a great fear that the Japanese would bomb the building if they discovered it. So they brought up a bunch of Hollywood set designers and made the entire roof look like a neighborhood, with fake houses, trees and roads. They even hired actors to walk up and down the fake sidewalks. Which led us to learn about the massive fake-out the Allies pulled on the Nazis before the invasion of Normandy. I printed out photos of fake ships, inflatable tanks and airplanes made of plywood that looked like the real thing from ten thousand feet up.

I also found stories of war dogs who both warned their humans of incoming artillery attacks and provided comfort in the foxholes. And stories of people like Irena Sendler, a Polish nurse who smuggled over two thousand children out of a Warsaw ghetto that was sealed off by the Nazis. She endured imprisonment and severe beatings and barely escaped execution. It was fascinating stuff.

Fern, who I adored, let me tell the story of her husband, Jim. She gave me some medals and papers to look at and the eulogy from his funeral said it all. It was written by one of his sons- "Dad told me he was getting an award for his service in the war and asked if I wanted to come up for the ceremony because he'd been awarded a Congressional Medal of Honor related to his service in the War. Apparently, he was a Tuskegee Airman…"

Jim had enlisted in the Army in March of 1941, six months before the bombing of Pearl Harbor. He wanted to fly planes, but because he was black and the armed forces were segregated, they sent him and a bunch of others down to Tuskegee, Alabama. They flew escorts to bombers and were so good the Red Tails, as they were called, were requested by the pilots of the B-17 bombers. And still, in typical American fashion, when they got home, these decorated pilots would be denied service at lunch counters all across the South. Jim served the duration of the war, and when he came home he didn't dwell on either the positives or the negatives of it, he went to school and got a degree in Social Work. He and Fern raised a few sons and he never talked about the war. His focus was all about raising his sons to become educated and contributing members of society.

The discussion group was such a hit I tried all kinds of other things, all with Gale's blessing. If they didn't work I just brushed them off and moved on to the next idea without a second thought. Manic energy can be good like that. I found most eighty year old ladies don't want to build a birdhouse, for instance, but some do like to watch you build a podium down in the activities room so you can start hosting Local Author Readings.

Ballard is full of writers, as is Seattle in general, and although it didn't work to have two writers a week come in, once or twice a month seemed to be plenty. We even had a couple major events, my favorite being when Peggy was a part of a nationally organized event called Listen To Your Mother, which, for the Seattle reading, was being held on a Saturday at Town Hall Seattle. Peggy was reading and convinced the other readers to do their practice run in our conference room the night before at exactly 6:30 pm. Some of them met for a drink beforehand and when they arrived a half hour later, they were told they were performing in front of a bunch of older ladies who were starting to get upset. If you learn nothing else in life, just know not to keep an eighty year old lady waiting.

The stories were written to be R-rated and a little racy and some of the readers looked terrified that they were about to read them in front of forty of their grandmothers. There was talk of vaginas and breasts sucked dry by greedy babies and plenty of foul language so I had to keep the doors closed, but I've never seen the residents laugh so hard and even if somebody had complained and I got in trouble, which didn't happen, it would have been well worth it.

For the election celebration, I put together a big party to celebrate the historic election of our first woman president. A couple residents were nervous about it but I assured everybody that Hillary was gonna win and there was absolutely nothing to worry about. There was NO WAY this country would ever elect that disgusting, petulant orangutan. I got wine for them and beer for me and I had the kitchen staff make up all kinds of snacks. I even invited over a bunch of my friends to be a part of it. Where better to watch election results than among a bunch of octogenarian ladies who had thought this day would never come?

I was out of beer about the time Florida got called and switched over to Three Buck Chuck, which was what we fed the residents. The residents left one by one, as did most of my friends. Serena stayed and I kept my hand on her leg, almost like it was grounding me from this New Atrocity. I did a quick clean up and went to the Market Arms for something stronger where I met up with our receptionist and bookkeeper. We drank until they closed and then went back to my boat and drank whisky until it was starting to get light. I got a call from Gale at nine asking if I was okay and if I needed to call in sick, like Dominique and Pat did. I dragged myself in, even though I was probably still drunk, but it was Wednesday, and Wednesdays are Doctor Run days.

The last run, on the worst day of my life, was Marie, who had a foot appointment. I loved Marie and we had become good friends. She and her husband built a couple houses many years ago and she knew all about finish work so we would sit in the library or lobby and criticize the moldings and sheetrock and talk about life. I spent more time with her than anybody because she was kind of a loner. She ate in her room and not the dining room because she had no use for whiny old ladies. But she always did all my events and I know that if we were the same age, we would have been lifelong friends, and I was sad when they signed her up for hospice.

When I picked up Marie for her ride home I was still feeling very strange. I was thoroughly hungover and may even have had a little alcohol poisoning, but I felt like something very deep inside me had changed, and not for the better. I got on Boren to get to Seneca and without bothering to think about it said, "Let's go into St James. It's right here. You can say a prayer for this fucked up country. I'll take you in. It won't take two minutes." She didn't want to go, even though she was catholic and you'd think she'd be wanting to say a couple Hail Marys or Our Fathers.

I tried to convince her that it would be good for her so I pulled over and got her walker out of the back. I found an open door and she's pretty slow so it took us a while to get into the cathedral. I half expected the place to be crowded but we were the only ones there so we sat in the front row. I told her if she wanted to kneel I'd help her but she just shot me a look and I thought she was stopping herself from swearing at me right there. She was probably saving it for when we got back to the car.

I was surprised that she, a life-long catholic, had no desire to be in what she must have considered to be a sacred place at such a critical time for our country. But I was mostly surprised that I, the leader of Scottish Buddhism, the staunchest of the atheistic religions, would feel a need to be in a place where I spent so many miserable hours in my childhood. After a couple of minutes, neither one of us was feeling it so we left.

When I had first started working at the Landmark, I told them I would work for a year at minimum wage and then they could re-evaluate my wage based on my performance. When they offered me a raise of one dollar an hour, I took it as a great insult. I didn't flat out quit because I genuinely liked most of the residents, but I told them to start looking for my replacement because I was going down to part-time. I left a little early that day and went for teriyaki and to send off a couple texts- one to Ryan from Ride the Ducks and one to former Captain Turner Loose.

Almost all of the Captains at Ride the Ducks had some kind of job or even a career outside of the Ducks. We had a local TV celebrity, Capt Noah Lott, two retired Navy helicopter pilots, Capt Rob R Ducky and Capt Beau Dayshus, and a guy who ran the drawbridges for the City of Seattle, Capt Turner Loose, also known as Greg.

Greg got right back to me and told me that a position just opened up on the bridges, but it starts part-time and it could be over a year before something full-time became available. And Ryan got back to me and said things were a lot different now at the Ducks but that I was welcome back. This was perfect because I was feeling drawn back to being a Duck Captain and thought I could do all three jobs, for three different reasons. The bridge job would be my security job, once I went full-time I could stay with it until I retired. The Duck job was for fun and cash during the tourist season. And the Landmark job would make me feel like I was doing something important, even if it was only for one or two days a week.

About a year after I left Ride the Ducks the first time, there had been a horrible accident in which five foreign students were killed and dozens of Duck passengers were injured. It closed operations for a while but the owners were determined to get up and running again. At the height of operations at Ride the Ducks we had twenty vehicles. Half were the original 1945 DUKW (Duck) surplus vehicles from WWII. The other half were reproductions built between the 1950's and the 1980's. Most of the other drivers preferred the reproductions because they rode better, and hated the original Ducks because they kept breaking down. But I always thought the original surplus DUKWs were cooler and I was alway sure to make my passengers aware that they were, kind of, maybe a little bit, connected to the Invasion of Normandy.

The accident happened on the Aurora Bridge when the front axle snapped on Duck 6 and sent it across the busy highway and right into a bus full of students and teachers from North Seattle College. Duck 6 was an original 1945 DUKW and never should have gotten onto Highway 99 and the busy Aurora Bridge in the first place. But it was up to the captain to decide how he or she got to the lake. We could go over the Aurora Bridge, which was great visually because you could see Mt Rainier and the snow-covered Cascades on the right and the Olympic mountains on the left. You're higher up in a Duck and can see over the railings of the bridge like you can't in a car and the view is spectacular. If you went over the Fremont Bridge to get to the lake you might have hit the drawbridge and been stuck for ten minutes or more depending on how far back you were. The Aurora bridge was scary but it was better for tips. The Fremont bridge was safer but you might have had to cut time off of the lake and that meant less of an experience. Whenever I think about the accident I always feel a little responsible because the Aurora Bridge was the route I always took.

The live image of the accident was broadcast all over the country and I got phone calls and texts from people who wanted to make sure that it wasn't me behind the wheel, even though I had left the Ducks over a year earlier. But looking at the live coverage on TV, which just kept showing the wreckage from different helicopter angles, I wasn't wondering 'What if that were me driving?', I was wondering, 'What if that bus hadn't been there?'. The body of the Duck isn't like a bus, it's actually a hull of a boat and has an upswept bow that could have easily cleared the meager side railing and dropped everybody onboard a hundred and fifty feet to the surface below. I wondered if that was one of the thoughts the Duck captain had between the time he lost both steering and brakes and the time the bus blocked his premature exit from the bridge.

Killed were a 17 year old from China, an 18 year old from Indonesia, a 20 year old from South Korea, a 36 year old from Japan and a 49 year old from Austria. Dozens of people, both on the North Seattle Community College bus and Duck 6 were injured.

Ride the Ducks shut down operations for several months and reopened with a lot of changes. First, of course, was no more highways and by extension, no more Aurora Bridge. Which made total sense when you realize that these DUKWs (at least the original ones, which were called Stretch Ducks) were designed to roll up onto beaches and transport supplies at no more than 20 MPH. All of the Stretch Ducks had to have their front axles replaced before they could drive again but as it turns out, business would be a fraction of what it was before the accident and the ten Truck Ducks (the newer reproduction Ducks), would be more than plenty to handle anybody still willing to ride a Duck.

But the biggest change was one that Ride the Ducks suggested before the Department of Transportation could. There would now be two people doing the tour, a tour guide whose job it was to entertain the guests, and the driver/captain whose only job would now be to safely drive around town and into the water without the distraction of talking to passengers, cuing up the music and changing goofy hats.

There were a few other changes, like going 5 MPH below all the posted speed limits, and cameras that recorded everything inside and outside the Duck. Ride the Ducks was now, probably, the safest commercial vehicle both on streets of Seattle and out on Lake Union. And since I had driven a Metro bus, a luxury coach, a trolley, a Ballard tour bus and a bus for a senior living facility, I always compared them in some way to driving a Duck. And when I told friends I was going back to being a Duck Captain again, I explained that the Ducks are back, like it or not, and it's better having a driver with a perfect safety record like me behind the wheel than some bozo, right?

SELF-MEDICATION

Self-medication sounds like something made up by an alcoholic bipolar person to justify his or her drinking but it's actually recognized by the psychiatric community, so there.

The body wants what the body wants and when it needs alcohol to calm its brain it's best just to give it to it. I need a few drinks at night to relax. It helps process what happened during the day and if for some reason I don't have a couple beers I will have a difficult time sleeping. When things are tough financially for me, which is more often than I like, I budget food and beer money equally, and make sure I always have my lithium.

I drink a fair amount and it's regular. I've also never quit drinking, even for a week and when my friends do a dry January, they do it alone. I don't ask them to quit taking their Advil and they don't ask me to give up my beer. The only time I ever curbed my drinking was when I went to nine beers a night but that was more about math. One night I'd get a twelve-pack, drink nine and the next day only have to get a six-pack. Math. Fortunately that was several years ago and my daily requirement has gone way down.

In the fifteen years I was with my wife, she never once accused me of drinking too much and when she finally left me, alcohol was not one of her reasons. I have never been late or called in sick to any job I've ever had. I have never been arrested (as an adult, anyway) or even pulled over for suspected DUI. I have a Class B commercial drivers license, a Captains license, been certified to operate drawbridges and a train, and had background checks performed by the City, the County and Federal government.

People self-medicate with coffee and all kinds of medication, of course, but the next time you see someone on the street strung out on drugs or piss drunk, consider there may be a serious untreated mental illness behind that and try to have a little understanding, if not empathy.

BACK ON MY MEDS

I asked my Mom and Dad if they could take Kenny for me as my life was about to get very busy since I was about to start working three different jobs. My parents were both newly retired so Kenny would have company all day long rather than being left alone on my boat seven days a week. Everybody wondered how Kenny would do without me because, as a rescue, he had attached himself to me like a tumor and never let me out of his sight. But I wasn't worried at all because my Dad's Parkinson's had been progressing and I knew Kenny would just attach himself to my Dad and forget all about me. That's just the kind of Cairn Terrier he is.

My Duck job wouldn't really kick in for a couple months because it was still the off-season, so that meant I could get all my training for the bridges out of the way. The City of Seattle operates five of the eight drawbridges in the city, with the State and a railroad operating the others. To get qualified to operate the bridges, you need to do thirty openings on each bridge while there's a certified bridge operator there talking you through it. It gets spread out over three days so that's ten openings per day. On the Fremont and Ballard bridges you can usually do all your practice openings for boats that want to pass, since the Fremont Bridge is supposedly the busiest drawbridge in North America and the Ballard Bridge is the second busiest. Ten openings in an eight hour shift is pretty common.

The three other bridges, the University Bridge, the Spokane Street Bridge and the South Park Bridge, however, may only open a couple times per shift so you need to do several openings without any actual boats present. And if you think people get mad when they get stuck by the bridge when they're already late for work, watch what happens when they get out of their car to see what's making them late and there's no boat there.

It seems like almost everybody who gets stuck by the bridge somehow thinks it's personal, as if the bridge tender saw them coming and they're paying them back for not being able to get them two weeks ago. Which is all perfectly understandable, since probably the most common human trait is the immediate ability to assume absolutely everything that happens around you is all about you.

Locals know that if you hit the bridge it's best to just turn off your engine and calm down. It will be over in less than five minutes, usually. There's no point in getting all worked up, turning around, and going to the Fremont Bridge because the boat that's going through the Ballard Bridge now will probably beat you there and you'll just end up waiting anyway.

When doing an opening with the canal bridges, especially the Fremont and Ballard bridges, it's all about timing. Any boat can request an opening but there are two factors that play into it every time- you can't make a boat wait more than ten minutes before starting an opening, and you can't keep the bridge open for more than ten minutes 'cause it messes up traffic. You can go all day with just one opening on the South Park Bridge but if you're on the Fremont Bridge you are constantly watching for what's coming next. You might have a sailboat approaching from the East and you're pretty sure they're gonna request an opening but you also see two other sailboats coming at you from the West, but they're spread out and if you do an opening too early the boat that's farthest away won't get there in time and you'll have to close it on him and you'll feel like a dick 'cause they'll have to wait two hours because the bridge doesn't open during morning and afternoon rush hours, so you give the first sailboat five short blasts of the horn which tells them they'll have to wait a little bit but then you get a call on the radio from a fishing boat that'll be there in five minutes and they're hoping for an opening 'cause it's 15:50 hours and they really want to also get through the Ballard Bridge before it, too, closes to boat traffic at 16:00 so they can get through the Locks and get home at a decent hour, so you try to do the math but math is hard and you say, Fuck It and start an opening and as soon as you do you see a bunch of drunks who've been sitting outside the Nickerson Street Saloon drinking cocktails all afternoon come rushing over to make the bridge and all of them dodge over or under the pedestrian gate but Becky can't seem to do it and now she's afraid 'cause the dude up in the tower, that's you, is yelling at her to get her ass off the gate and she's somehow both laughing and drunk crying and finally she just sits on the ground waiting for the SWAT team to show up and she starts telling a guy on a bike she's about to get shot but finally all the pedestrian gates are down and just as you hit the STOP light for the cars, you hear a siren in the distance so you close the gates for the oncoming cars but leave the gates up for the offgoing cars so the firetruck or ambulance can still get around the gates and you wait for what feels like a WHOLE MINUTE for the emergency vehicle to show up and when it does it goes down Westlake instead of the bridge so you lower the offgoing gates and everybody hates the ass-hole up in the tower who yells at young ladies and makes them wait in their boats and cars but you start the opening and pretty soon this will be over and you'll have two hours between 16:00 and 18:00 hours when there will be no openings 'cause it's a weekday and you can eat your dinner and do the crossword and just as the leafs are coming down and you're almost done the far leaf stops so, in addition to panicking, you start to raise the far leaf again separately and manually instead of together and automatically with the near leaf and you don't pray 'cause praying's stupid but you're REALLY

FUCKING HOPING this works because you hate paperwork and if the bridge gets stuck and the mechanics have to come out you're probably gonna get shot by a commuter so you take a breath and close the blinds and you start to drop the far leaf and it goes all the way down and you engage the center locking pin and raise all the gates and turn on the green lights and log the opening and sit down and hope that will be the worst opening of the day.

The next day, you might be on the South Park Bridge and your biggest concern might be that if you watch all the Netflix shows you got going there won't be anything left to watch at home on your night off.

One of the first thoughts I had when I first got the bridge job was that it would be a great way for me to start writing again. It had just self-published my cookbook and although I wasn't ready for a whole new book, maybe it would be worth it to start a blog. There was another bridge tender, Barb, that had a blog that the supervisors knew about, so it must be okay. Her blog is good but it's got absolutely nothing to do with being a bipolar bridge tender, so both blogs could easily coexist. I tried to get the domain name offmymeds.com but somebody had already claimed it and wanted over $4,000 for it! So instead I got backonmymeds.com, which was probably smarter anyway, as the idea of an openly bipolar bridge operator might bring the wrong kind of attention, especially seeing how sensitive commuters are.

I get all my domain names from the same place and every time I get a new one I'm confronted with the dozen or more pointless ones that I already have. I started my blog, backonmymeds.com but also got the domain name, scottishbuddhism.com which I directed to the same site, thinking it could be kind of a main site for my other stuff. I have a website for my book, scottishbuddhistcookbook.com, and two for my bagpipes, pipefetish.com and craigpipes.com. I've got one for my tiny house, itsaportablecabin.com, and a non-profit I meant to start about helping people build their own portable cabins called steptwoseattle.com. I've got ballardart.com 'cause I started doing oil paintings, and ballardbell.org that I thought I would make a website for but just directed to the Ballard Historical Society instead.

I recently got elmerfisher.com so I can put together an all-in-one database for him and his work and I thought it would be cool to have some kind of interactive walking tour or something of his buildings. I also had to get braveliver.net because braveliver.com was taken. Not by somebody who has any intention of using it, but by somebody who thinks I'm gonna pay him five fucking thousand dollars for it. I've had a few others over the years but I just usually let them expire, like microhouseboat.com. and ballardwriters.com. For some reason, though, I still have qualitysouls.com.

Back around the time of Huggy Jesus, a good fifteen years earlier, Sean and I were talking one day about souls. Being a Scottish Buddhist, I think the idea of a person having a soul that lives on after them is ridiculous. It doesn't make any sense and the idea of being conscious for all eternity sounds like the worst kind of hell imaginable. But Sean felt like people had to have souls because that's what separates us from the animals.

"So King didn't have a soul?", I asked, remembering him telling me about his exceptionally smart dog who he would take with him when he would steal cocaine from Miami drug lords.

"Well, dogs, sure..."

"What about cats?" Sean was now collecting feral cats. Of course he would think they would have a soul.

"I'm just saying people have souls. Maybe not you, Jayhawk, but normal people have souls."

"So if you have a soul, it's yours to do what you want with it...?" I was starting to get an idea. "I'll give you twenty dollars for your soul right now." He shrugged and didn't even counteroffer. Either he didn't think his soul was worth more than $20 or he really needed some smokes and didn't want to risk blowing the deal.

I wrote up a contract that Sean and I both signed and I showed it to Steven the next time he came by. It seemed so simple and brilliant we couldn't understand why this wasn't already a thing. Pretty much every single religion, probably, thinks people have souls, that's part of how they get their members. Most people throughout history have hoped that their consciousness would live on after their bodies have stopped living, so that's gotta be worth something. And there are all these old stories about people selling their souls to the devil so it's not a crazy idea.

Let's say, for example, you went downtown with a bunch of twenties and a stack of Certificates of Ownership cards with the SIN (Soul Identification Number) already on them. You could buy a couple dozen souls in an afternoon, easy. It would probably be smart to offer a short grace period in case they change their mind and need to get their soul back for its agreed upon value. With a small processing fee, of course.

Once we had amassed a bunch of souls we would go about selling them for a nice profit. I imagined somebody who had done some questionable things in their life might be up for buying a few extra souls, just in case it helps them on Judgement Day. Who knows? Or maybe some retiree in Kansas might just want to collect them in case they're worth something someday. Again, who knows? But the big money would probably be in celebrities who were down on their luck. You just gotta catch the Danny Bonaduces and Tonya Hardings of the world at the exact right time and you could make a killing.

I envisioned owning a kind of a database that would establish the Soul Identification Number as the standard in the brokering of human souls and allowing other people, there would surely be others, to be brokers. But as other people got in they would have to register to get a certified SIN from us, for only $5 a pop, otherwise they wouldn't have any legitimacy. Once they had that they could buy and sell as many souls as they want.

I bought soulregistrar.com to be the official repository of souls, and I felt relieved that the name was still available. It's always nice when you have a brilliant idea and nobody's beaten you to the domain name. Next, I got a bunch of domain names to be brokers of souls and I wanted them to be reflective of what people were looking for, so I got qualitysouls.com, which I still have for some reason, soulsforless.com, soulsforjesus.org (you do not have to be a non-profit to get a .org, by the way), heathensouls.com, savemysoul.net, and a couple like soulporn.com, I can't remember them all. Steven also bought a bunch of them but he's probably let them all lapse by now, too.

Steven and I have always been big proponents of the Two Beer Rule, in that all business decisions and strategies should never even be considered until after two beers. There's probably no scientific basis for it, but it just feels right. The only problem with the Two Beer Rule is that it often turns into two beers, several more beers, a couple vodka martinis or margaritas, a few whiskys and then some more beers. Which can make starting up something like this even harder than it should be. Plus, neither one of us wanted to front it. I thought he would be perfect 'cause he already had a huge base of Utilikilt customers and he was evil, but he thought I should be the one to do it. I had Sean fronting the Huggy Jesus thing, so I was safe there, but I was saving myself for Huggy Mohammed which was going to be a dog chew toy, and that was enough exposure for me. So nothing ever happened with the soul venture. Or Huggy Mohammed, for that matter.

DEALING WITH MANIC DEPRESSION ONLY GETS EASIER

When I first got diagnosed with bipolar disorder it felt like I only had a few years left in me. My best friend had just died and I took it way too hard, my wife left me because she couldn't take the manic episodes, and my business was doomed. My first psychiatrist was throwing all kinds of drugs at me to see what worked. In the first few years I went from deep depressions to soaring highs and it was exhausting. There's no way I could do that now.

And for everything I've learned about medications and making the bed every day, the most important thing to know is that dealing with manic depression only gets easier. As long as you work on it. And you will have to work on it. Every day.

I think the biggest thing that helped me early on when I was either depressed or manic was realizing that I had been there before and I got out of it. It always seems like it's worse than it's ever been and there's no way of getting out of it this time, but even that feeling becomes familiar.

Being bipolar is like having a full-time job on top of a part-time job but after several years it gets easier. And for all the bad that comes with it, there are good things, too. The manic energy, when used for good, is fun. The feelings of euphoria are fun. The strong emotional feelings you have make you very empathetic, which makes you a better person, but the downside is that you now unexpectedly cry at TV commercials.

Being bipolar just means you are capable of great things, like rebuilding a city or making bagpipes, whether anybody appreciates it or not.

Life is short and you can never really appreciate the ups without the downs and if you have been diagnosed as bipolar, you're a step ahead of most people.

WHALES!!!!

My friend Karen organized a yoga retreat for the Summer Solstice in Ketchikan. I don't do yoga but Laura and Peggy and a few other Ballardites were going and I've always wanted to go to Alaska. It was going to be at a fishing lodge on an island off the coast and my first thought was- Whales!!!!

I asked for two weeks off but Ride the Ducks said No because they never had enough captains this time of year and it sucks turning away customers. I told Trisha I was sorry but that this was something I was doing. I didn't threaten to quit because I don't believe in threats, you either do something or you don't. But I reminded her that in the four years I had been at Ride the Ducks I had never taken a vacation, never even used a sick day. Ever. Which was pretty remarkable because it seemed everybody else called in sick once a week and if you were On Call you could pretty much count on having to cover somebody's shift 'cause they just weren't 'feeling it' that day or wanted to go fishing instead of driving Stormy Weathers or Sonny Daze around for ten painful hours.

I moved to Seattle in 1996 and have never, not once, seen a whale here. My first apartment had a porch overlooking Elliott Bay and I spent hours looking for the orcas, humpbacks or gray whales that supposedly ran through several times a year but I never saw a single one. It seemed like every other asshole in Seattle has seen a whale from the beach or out on a ferry but not me, so my one and only goal for this yoga retreat was to see a whale and I told my friends that I wasn't coming home until I saw one.

Years ago, after my wife left me, I started talking to my friend Teresa who I knew from the Dutch Tavern back in New London, CT. She was now a school teacher living in Boston but we always got along well and there was definitely some attraction going on, even though nothing ever happened. But now with Vanessa gone, things were different. I went back to Boston for a visit and for her Christmas she would come to Seattle. I told her to bring her passport 'cause I got us a hotel room up in Victoria for a few days.

The day before she came out, a local TV station did a story about Huggy Jesus, the stuffed Jesus doll Sean and I developed that was sure to make us rich. My friend Joe set us up with a website and a way to sell these dolls through something called zShop, which was Amazon's failed first attempt to let everyday people sell their shit online. It was about a week before Christmas and we only had a couple dozen dolls ready to ship and it would take a few weeks to get a bunch more made so we made some cards with a photo of Huggy Jesus and His outstretched arms with "I AM COMING!" underneath that we could send out to tide people over.

As soon as the TV piece aired we got bombarded with orders and I watched them pile up one after the other every time I refreshed my computer screen. It was Glorious. There are many ways to get rich in this world but what better way to do it than off Jesus?

The next morning I saw that the orders had stopped and it appeared that my account had crashed. I picked Teresa up at the airport and explained what happened and that I needed to stay and deal with it. I put her on the Victoria Clipper and told her I'd be up the next day. I spent all day trying to get through to somebody at the zShop office but it turns out they had all gone off for their goddamn Christmas vacation and there was nobody to reset my account to start accepting orders again. I was furious, then disappointed, then trying desperately to appreciate the irony of it when Teresa called from the hotel room in Victoria. She was so excited she could barely get it out.

"I got in the room, which is great, by the way, and I turned on the TV and the Canadian CNN was on and you wouldn't believe what they were showing! They picked up the Huggy Jesus story and they were talking about it! You're gonna be rich! And guess what else! You'll never believe this! The ferry, which is awesome by the way, you'll love it, had to come to a complete stop 'cause there were a bunch of orcas! They completely surrounded the ferry! There were so many of them and they were sticking their heads out and I swear to God you probably could have touched one of them! I wasn't gonna try but I know you probably would have, honey! Oh my God it was so exciting! I can't wait til you're up here! Did you fix the problem with your Jesus doll?"

I had not fixed the problem with my Jesus doll. All I had was a bunch of pissed off people and a lost opportunity. Maybe I could regroup for Easter but I was already dreading what THAT would look like and on top of everything I didn't get to see my whales. Teresa sees whales up close on her first full day in Seattle while I've been looking for them for five goddam years and I was starting to wonder if maybe I was wrong. Maybe there IS a God and He's a fucking asshole! Now THAT makes sense!

So when, some fifteen years later and I still hadn't seen a single whale, I had the opportunity to go up to Alaska to hunt whales, there was no way I wasn't going. It's not like the Ducks were gonna fire me just as the season was starting. Since I came back I was otherwise a model employee so I was sure they would get over it.

Ketchikan is a great town and this was my first real vacation in many years so I'm sure I had a smile on my face the whole time. It's a small place and the waterfront is set up for all the cruise ships that come in and that part's kind of gross. All the passengers get off the ships for a couple hours and buy their trinkets from stores that are owned by the cruise lines and don't usually get into the actual town at all, which is a shame 'cause Ketchikan is awesome.

We had a couple days in Ketchikan before going out to the fishing lodge where the yoga retreat was and I knew there had to be at least a few traditional Alaskan dive bars. I found the Sourdough Bar pretty quick and went in to relax and check my phone for emails.

"Hey! Asshole!", I heard as I walked by the guys sitting at the bar. Oh fuck, I'm getting into a bar fight on my first night in Alaska.

Some big and obviously very drunk fisherman type came over to my table and slurred, "You can't just walk in here in your kilt, and you're pretty hair", he patted my head, "and sit alone! You're gonna come sit with me and I'm gonna buy you drinks! Come over here with me, asshole!" I don't remember walking back to the hotel at all.

The whole area around Ketchikan is an actual temperate rainforest and there are a ton of islands off the coast. Our fishing lodge was only a twenty minute boat ride away but I sure felt like I was a thousand miles away from anything. I packed in lots of beer and wine, which pound for pound, is still the safest way to travel if you have a hard time limiting your scotch intake. I know food insecurity is a real thing for way too many people, but alcohol insecurity is just as real to people like me so I can endure the judgy looks.

I set up a little writing area in the corner of the yoga room by the window so I could look out across the narrow channel and watch for whales. We saw some orcas a couple times and we all ran down to the dock to gawk at them, but they were pretty far away. Since it was a fishing lodge there were some 16' dinghies with outboard motors and we were free to use them any time so I went out hunting whales a couple times a day, but never saw any up close.

As the week was winding down we decided to motor out to what was supposed to be an abandoned village tucked away in a small inlet called Loring. There was once a couple hundred people living there but now there were only five or six left. Like most of coastal Alaska there are no ways in except by boat or seaplane, so they don't get many visitors and we were probably their first yoga tourists from Seattle. Laura knocked on doors until she found Leonard, who'd lived there for almost his whole life and who was happy to give us the skinny on this ghost town that was once Ketchikan's competitor. Afterwards we got in the boats and headed back to the lodge for Happy Hour. Just as we were getting back and about to dock, one of the lodge dudes said that somebody spotted some whales just going around the South side of the island. I had Laura and Karen in my boat and Peggy had Anna in hers.

About halfway up the West side of the island I saw a fluke about a thousand feet off and after getting closer and watching for a while, we could see a pattern. They would all rise up out of the surface and hang out for a minute, then disappear for about five or ten minutes and then resurface a few hundred feet North. I was getting us closer and watching and guessing where they might surface next.

They were remarkably close to the shore and I realized that's because the water is really deep there, like several hundred feet deep, just a couple hundred feet offshore. Crazy deep and cold and dark and instant death if you get beneath the surface.

There were four humpbacks and they were doing something I later learned was a bubble net, which is where a group of whales circle around a school of fish and blow bubbles and corral them into a tight ball and then take turns coming up from beneath and gorging themselves on the herring or other small fish. Once we got closer we could figure out what they were doing and I made a guess as to where they would surface next. I drove to a spot that I thought was where they would come up and cut the engine to drift and wait. It was like a game of darts where you aim for the center and hope you still just get in the circle. If we got within two hundred feet I would be thrilled. We were each facing in different directions looking for signs of bubbles and I saw Peggy standing in her boat waving her arms and yelling something at us when bubbles started coming up around our boat and fish started jumping and I realized that the whales were circling right under us.

There was nothing to do but watch as they came up not even thirty feet off our starboard side. There were bubbles and fish and the water seemed to heave up and then the water became mouths full of water and fish and bubbles and the mouths were whales and then the whales closed their mouths and slowly fell back down into the water as we watched speechless with our own mouths hanging open like we just saw the most amazing thing we could ever see.

The four humpbacks stayed on the surface for a bit, taking in and expelling air and then slowly, gracefully raised their flukes and slipped back under the surface. Karen asked, "Should we be afraid right now?", and Laura and I looked at each other, thought about it and both agreed that, nah, we're fine. We drifted around a bit and we thought it would be nice if we gave them a head start before heading back over the top of the island, when the water swelled again between us and the shore. We were just talking about how that was the coolest thing we'll ever see for the whole rest of our lives when one of the whales looked at us, rolled over and made a deep loud noise that was clearly some kind of message. It was either that we are all inhabitants of this beautiful world and we all have a place here in it and peace and love, or, you got way too freaking close and we almost killed your dumb asses.

Back at the room I was so full of adrenaline I didn't stand a chance of sleeping. I drank beer and wine and paced back and forth until it was daylight and then I went out and stood on the shore and realized that no matter how long I live, I would never experience anything like that again. The thought was a little depressing but it did help bring me back down just a little bit.

WHY TO BUILD A TINY HOUSE

I lived on an old wooden boat in the Ballard neighborhood of Seattle for over ten years and it probably saved my life. After the traumatic death of my buddy Dave, my then-wife dragged me into a psychiatrist and I began my experiment with several kinds of medication. Uppers to treat my depression and downers to treat my mania, which seemed only to amplify my bipolar disorder.

After my wife left me I also lost my business and my apartment. I drifted in and out of homelessness a few times before managing, with the help of my friend and ex-partner, Paul, who gave me boatwork when he had it, to buy a boat to live on. I kept it at a small marina next to the Ballard Locks and I always felt like I was getting away with something and that it could end at any moment. How could it be that I could be living in my own home, in the best neighborhood in Seattle, for only a few hundred dollars a month?

Living on an old wooden boat comes with a price, though. There's the walking down the dock wondering if your home had sunk while you were at work. Would it drop to the bottom and rip out all the cleats or would the cleats hold long enough for you to get your cairn terrier out? And you have to sleep with one ear open, constantly listening for the bilge pumps kicking on more than usual or some new ominous influx of water. But still, it beat the hell out of a $1,500 a month apartment.

It was my incredibly low overhead combined with a marina owner who let me slide for several months through long periods of rapid-cycling that kept me from living on the street and eventually taking my own life. I never think about killing myself when I'm manic because there's too much I have to do. And I may think about suicide when I'm depressed but it just seems like too much effort and I've learned to just ride out the depression 'cause it always passes, eventually.

Rapid-cycling can start out as a period of mania followed by a period of depression, followed by much shorter periods of mania and depression, followed by a couple weeks of being manically depressed. This is by far the worst state for me to be in. I can't sleep for days, I hate myself and my life, my brain won't shut off, and it saps everything out of me. I've read that the average life expectancy of somebody with manic depression is ten to twenty years less than those without it, and it's my guess that many if not most suicides by bipolar people happen while rapid-cycling. It wasn't until I found Katie, who put me on lithium, that I was finally able to level out. I still had my ups and downs but they were manageable and not nearly as severe. I had finally found a little peace and a sense of normalcy. I still bounced from job to job but at least I had a place to go home to every night.

And then Bill sold the marina, adding a whole new level of insecurity into my life. The new owners came in and required everybody to get insurance and register their vessels, which is easier said than done with an old wooden liveaboard. And none of the other marinas in Seattle still allowed old wooden liveaboards because they are both fire hazards and constantly in danger of sinking. So I was fucked.

I knew somebody who worked for an insurance company so I was able to get insurance without having to haul my boat out for an inspection. All I had to do was sneak onto another boat and take some pictures of their nice, dry bilge and pretend it was mine. But I couldn't get it registered 'cause I couldn't find the title or come up with a fake one that was believable. So I decided it was time to appreciate the ten years I had had and move on to something with some security.

My first thought was to build an actual houseboat. Something with a fiberglass hull that any marina would fall over themselves welcoming to their docks. I made a few scale models and created a website and Facebook page titled Micro Houseboat. If I could build two for other people, the third one, mine, would pay for itself. I spent $1,000 on lumber, screws and other materials to build a jig that I could build an unlimited number of houseboat hulls on. It was 32' long by 8' wide, but could come apart into four pieces, just in case I didn't have any orders and had to store it for a bit.

I never got any orders so I had to store it and come up with a better plan. First, I thought of taking an old Ford van and turning it into an amphibious vehicle that I could live in, either on land or water. This seemed to make the most sense because a buddy of mine had six or eight of these vans at his shop already, and I could get one cheap and convert it there in his yard while I lived out of it. The logistics of keeping the motor dry didn't make sense, ultimately, so my friend suggested I just get a box van.

I had exactly $5,000 to my name and right away found a 17' Uhaul box truck on CraigsList. The description was very thorough but I was nervous about driving the forty miles on my bike to look at it. I sent him a picture of five thousand dollars in cash and told him if he can drive it up to Seattle tonight I'll give him all of it, as is. It was in perfect condition and even every little clearance light at the top of the box worked properly, telling me this was well-maintained.

I gave my boat away to the first person who was willing to take on the liability of an old wooden boat with no title and moved my new box van to my friend's shop to begin living in it. There wasn't much to move, mostly clothes, a few bagpipes and whatnot. About half of what I owned went into the dumpster and there was no furniture because a boat's furniture is built in.

With my new box truck I thought briefly of starting a Scottish Buddhist moving company where we toss out half your shit and curse at you the whole time for being so materialistic, but realized that probably wouldn't fly here in Seattle.

I stopped at Fred Meyer to get an air mattress and then into the yard where I would spend the next couple years turning my box van into what I now call a Portable Cabin. Along the way I learned a couple things, which you might want to know if you're thinking of living in the back of a Uhaul.

HOW TO BUILD A PORTABLE CABIN

Make a bathroom. You need a toilet and a shower. Thinking you'll just live next to some facilities is both lazy and ignorant. Building a bathroom is Job #1.

Forget about making the 'Mom's Attic' space over the cab into a sleeping loft. It's way too small. Besides, it makes a great place for your water and electrical systems and some storage.

Get used to using cast iron pans and nonstick pots that don't require a lot of water to clean. You will not have a dishwasher (or a washer and dryer, for that matter) but your water consumption will be a fraction of the normal American, which is not only laudable in itself but it gives you something to talk about at family gatherings.

Build bump-outs that can slide in, like on those fancy RVs. Next to the bathroom, the greatest thing about my portable cabin is the bump-out for the bed. The head of the bed sticks out of the side about three feet and it has a skylight. I see stars above me at night, I wake up with the sun, and I love it when it pounds down rain. I also have a bump-out for the stove and oven and another for a pantry.

Get some solar panels. It's surprisingly cheap now to go solar. You can still run an extension cord for a fridge or small heater, but you need at least a 200 watt system for the DC power, which includes the shower's water pump, fan for the propane fireplace, safety switches for the propane, lights, etc.

Build a rain collector. An 8'x10' rain collector and 30 gallon tank can provide you with free showers for a couple weeks between rainy days. Also you'll need to learn how to take short showers.

Embrace propane. Install safety switches for each propane tank and you can have cheap, safe energy for your cooking, heat, shower, and even your fridge if you're willing to shell out over $1,000 for a refrigerator. My shower uses less than gallons of propane a year. That's less than $40/year for a shower every day. I'm killing it.

Use repurposed materials whenever you can. I turned an old bowling alley locker into a horizontal storage unit and found a great solid mahogany door with leaded glass for a hundred bucks.

Take off the roll-up door and build a proper entrance. With a porch. And a place for a grill.

Insulate. One of the best things about converting a Uhaul into a portable cabin is that it's super easy to insulate. You can insulate the floor and ceiling and still have over seven feet of headroom. And you can do the side insulation when putting on the siding and not lose any interior space.

COMPOST MENTIS

Space is limited when you start building a tiny house so you can be forgiven for giving a quick thought to not including a bathroom to your living space. Maybe you think you'll just park next to a place that has a toilet or that you can just carry a bucket for emergencies. But life doesn't work that way. You might think somebody else's toilet will always be available or that shitting in a bucket in an emergency isn't so bad but you'll realize soon enough that your new tiny home is pretty worthless without a toilet.

One of the first questions a person has when they step inside your tiny house or portable cabin is, How do you go to the bathroom? It's unfair, of course, because if you ask that when you walk into somebody's regular-sized house they look at you funny. But it's a fair question for a portable cabin and when you bring a guest home for the first time it can be a definite deal breaker.

The bathroom is its own separate room, containing the shower, toilet and medicine cabinet. There's no sink but there is a shelf for hand-sanitizer and the shower nozzle is right there and there's a sink in the kitchen just five feet away. It measures three feet by eight feet, the width of the Uhaul. The shower insert is 3' x 3' and it's perfectly fine. The composting toilet is built-in and is three feet wide and about two feet deep. It is supremely nicer than the head that was in my 35' Chris Craft.

I built the floor up about four inches which worked well because it reinforces that you are entering into a separate room, and it was very worth it. I thought I didn't need a door but then I had a visitor and she made me cover my head with a pillow and sing the National Anthem before I remembered that women are funny about bathroom stuff. It's a hard enough sell for some people to use a composting toilet for the first time so you're definitely gonna need a door.

The boat that I lived on for over ten years had a holding tank for the toilet, as required. RVs also have a holding tank but I was adamant about not having one because you have to pay to get them pumped out and it's a hassle and no matter what you do, they are going to stink. They make chemicals that they tell you will cut down on the smell but all they do is add a chemical smell to the fecal sludge, which is just as disgusting.

They make a composting toilet called the Nature's Head, which has been around for a long time. It's $950 and they're the main composting toilet for boaters. Being a Scottish Buddhist there is no way I'm dumping that kind of money into something I'll be shitting in so I researched how they actually work so I could make my own.

There are several ideas on how to best compost human waste, but there is one thing that is a constant- you have to separate the liquids from the solids. The pee from the poo. There is a diverter that works for both males and females and everything in between. It is situated to collect the urine and divert it to a separate container. The solids fall straight down into a larger compartment where they are mixed with a composting agent, like peat or coconut fiber. In many cases the solids are dried out using heat and aeration. I made several variations before settling on a method that is efficient, cost-effective, essentially odorless, and by far the easiest to maintain. I call it the Craigger. My branch of the Craig name will die with my sister (she's younger and never gets those 'suicidal

ideations') so there needs to be something that lives on. This is
how the Craigger (no patent pending) and the shower work-

The toilet is basically a wood box with a standard toilet seat
on top, the diverter positioned under the front, and a five gallon
bucket. I buy compostable plastic bags to use as liners so it's super
easy to change. I made it so the toilet seat pops off easily and I can
grab the used bag and put a fresh one in in just seconds.

I attached a hose from the diverter that runs outside so there is
never urine in my house. The idea of a bunch of urine festering in
a person's living space completely grosses me out. I keep a jug of
water next to the toilet and dump a little in to flush the diverter and
hose so it doesn't smell.

The diluted urine goes outside and into a flower box that is full of
succulents, pansies, wheatgrass and other hardy, non-edible plants.
Urine, I've learned, is full of nutrients like nitrogen, potassium and
phosphorus and instead of dumping it all down into a sewer system
or into a septic tank, why aren't more people doing this, especially

since we always seem to be in a goddamn water crisis? The average person pees about a half-gallon of urine a day, and uses anywhere from **six to thirty gallons** of perfectly good water to flush it down. I use maybe a quart of collected rainwater per day in my Craigger.

The urine goes through the upper hose and then aims into a funnel that is open so when it rains the lower hose gets flushed out even more. I put a bunch of holes in the lower hose to distribute the diluted urine the length of the box and although I haven't seen a single example of somebody else doing this, it works perfectly.

Maintaining the solid waste is almost as easy. I buy a 50-count box of 13-gallon composting bags for about $16 which lasts about three months, and I get sawdust from my table saw. I throw the sawdust in first and then add more whenever I use it. Toilet paper goes right in, as well as whatever you want to compost. When I take the bag out, I tie it off and throw it in a paper bag and toss it in the garbage and consider it 'neutral waste'. It will go into a landfill and in a year or so it will just be dirt. I do not and will not ever consider using my waste to fertilize growing vegetables, that's disgusting.

I got the urine diverter from Johnny Compost on Etsy for about fifty bucks and had everything else kicking around. If you had to buy some plywood, lumber for the flower box, hoses and whatnot, you could spend a couple hundred bucks. But it's a fuckload cheaper than a Nature's Head and you'll never have to empty a piss pot.

My shower wasn't as cheap but I did it at the same time as I installed my solar system so it felt a lot more expensive. The shower is completely off-grid and I have never gone without a shower, even if the neighborhood has lost power or water. It's beautiful.

I use rain water, solar power and propane. My rain collector is 8' x 10' and it's just 2x4s and that cheap corrugated plastic roofing from Home Depot and a gutter. If you're not tying into a larger solar system you'll need a 100 watt solar panel and a twelve volt battery ($150) to power the water pump. The on-demand propane hot water heater will run you $300, the shower stall about $250, water tank $200 and with all the little things, you're approaching $1,000. Still totally worth it.

The rain lands on the collector and drops into the gutter and then into a tray that's attached to a 1" plastic pipe. The pipe runs to a filter and then inside and into the water tank. You'll need to make a vent/drain at the top of the tank so excess water goes outside, maybe even into another tank. My tank is only fifteen gallons because it's just what I had but you'll want a thirty gallon tank if you can get one. On the bottom of the tank you'll run a hose to the water pump and from there another hose to the water heater.

You'll need a three-gallon-per minute, 12 volt water pump (about $80), an inline strainer, an on/off knob and the proper wiring. I mounted my water heater and on/off switch just next to the shower and everything else is in the forward locker.

The propane tank is in its own locker that I access from the outside. As with all the propane tanks you use, install a safety solenoid at the tank with a switch inside. When the switch is off, no propane can get inside the living space. I'm not sure if RVs use these safety switches but they're mandatory on boats.

There are a few ways of dealing with the waste water. One way is to have a gray water tank that you can also use for your galley sink but the problem with that is that now you have something you need to pump out. What I do is much easier and less impactful. I made a filter out of a large milk crate that I line with paper bags and fill with crumpled up newspaper. The water passes through and leaves the soap scum and all I have to do is swap out the bags every so often. The other thing I do is only use biodegradable soaps. I just use a bar of Ivory soap in the shower and biodegradable dish soap in the galley.

My showers are only as long as they need to be and I use about two gallons of rainwater. I use recycled, compostable paper plates and clean my non-stick pots and pans and silverware with a vinegar and water mixture as I go so it doesn't take much water to finish cleaning them. I still have to use an off-site washer and dryer, but still, my water usage is a fraction of yours.

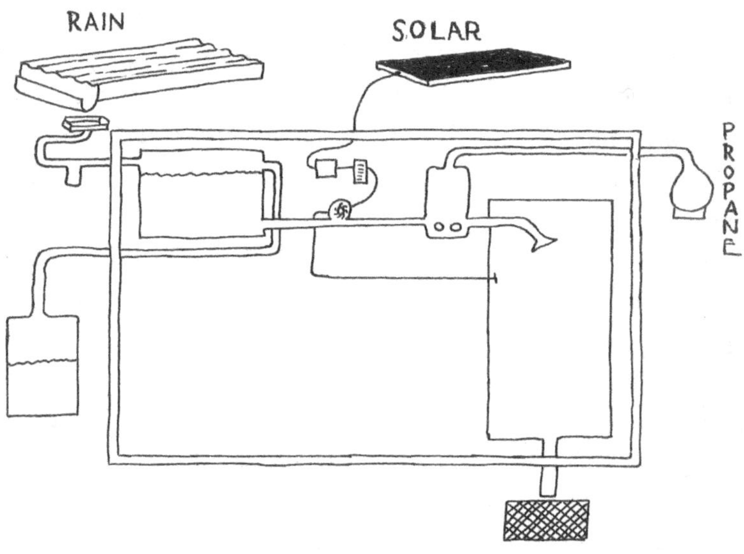

THE FENPRO

The Fenpro building was my favorite building in Seattle. It was massive, yet you could somehow pass by it without ever noticing it, as I'm sure countless visitors to the Locks or Shilshole have done since it first started taking shape after World War Two.

There was a shipyard on the canal and they owned a large yard on the other side of the tracks up to Market Street that they used for storage, mostly. But then they started putting up outbuildings for different things and they erected a block-long wall along the street to both keep people out and stop them from looking in. From then on, it was just a mishmash of purpose-built buildings of every size and construction. And since it was just a yard, technically, there were never any building permits and no building inspectors. When the Fire Department came around, everybody knew to just lay low and pop a beer or smoke a bowl until they went away.

I forget the details but there were two blocks of buildings owned by two brothers who turned the property into a huge aluminum extrusion business. They made windows for skyscrapers and sign posts for highways and aluminum fishing boats and all kinds of things until they had a falling out and split up in the 1990's. The Fentron building became home to a Habitude day spa, the Kiss Cafe, and a few other proper businesses while the Fenpro became a haven for industrial craftsmen, artists, glassblowers, etc, etc, etc, etc and etc.

It's also where I went from being a stressed-out business owner to a worry free, employee-less bagpipe maker that did odd jobs to survive. My shop was big enough to build a boat hardtop in if I had to, but was really more about a lathe, bench sanders and other tools for making Great Highland bagpipes out of brass, fiberglass, carbon fiber, and driftwood. It was very good for my mental health. Or very bad, it's hard to tell sometimes.

The Fenpro was the perfect home for me. It wasn't really just one building, it was actually dozens and dozens of makeshift buildings built next to, on top of and inside each other. I once counted about eighty separate shops and artist studios and figured there were about two hundred people who either worked there full time or kept a studio there. The activity was nonstop with somebody, somewhere, always working on something. One of the late night denizens was Denny who had escaped Iowa several years earlier and brought a deep knowledge of how to heat and bang metal until it did what he wanted it to do. Most of his work was brought to him by artists who had gotten grants to make some big metal sculptures and needed somebody to actually build them. His work is all over the place but it's usually uncredited and he never took photos of the finished product, which I could totally relate to. After spending several frustrating months with an artist who has little understanding of how a metal sculpture is actually made, it's sometimes easier to just walk away and pretend it never happened.

For over ten years I was at the Fenpro just about every day. First with my bagpipe shop and then at Denny's shop, either working on a project with him or just coming over with some beer or bourbon to hang out and swap stories. When I get depressed I try to make an effort to get out and be around other people and that started with Denny. My boat was just behind the Fenpro in the last dumpy marina in Seattle and before I found Dr Katie, all I had to do was grab a twelve pack and Kenny and I would go to Denny's shop to hang out for a while. It wasn't quite as effective as lithium but it helped.

There had been talk for years that the Fenpro building was being sold to make way for the new Nordic Heritage museum because their current location, an old school that they'd been renting for a dollar a year, was falling apart and the City was taking it back. The museum took it as an opportunity to raise a bunch of money and build what they said would be the biggest Nordic Heritage museum outside of all of Scandinavia. Everybody at the Fenpro was horrified, of course, but we all held out hope that they wouldn't be able to raise the $40 million or whatever they said a museum like that would take. When asked my opinion by a reporter I said the whole idea was terrible, not only because it would upend a couple hundred people who had nowhere else to go, including myself, but because there was no way it would be successful. Nobody's going to pay money to get into a Norwegian museum! If they want to make it interesting, I told her, make it a Scottish museum. THAT would be interesting.

As the new Nordic museum prepared to demolish the Fenpro building, several of us started to organize a farewell party and Abby, who'd been taking pictures of the neighborhood for years, brought her old-school tri-color camera inside to get some last photos before everything was gone. We planned a farewell bash to show off just a taste of the huge range of projects that had come out of the building over the years, but then at the last minute, even after hanging Abby's posters all over Ballard, the property managers forbade us from doing anything. So we hung signs telling people we got shut down and went into the section where Lyle was building an Alaskan fishing boat to have a private party there instead.

Lyle was one of the top hip surgeons in the country (I knew this not because he told me but because I looked it up) and he was building a boat from scratch with his old friends from high school. It took them about four years and Lyle could have just bought a boat, but this was their therapy project. Every Saturday they'd come in about 11am, figure out what they'd be doing, and then go across the street to the Sloop for beer and burgers. They'd get about five or six hours of work done and then go home happy. Some people like to go to the beach or hiking for fun, and some people, like those who rented space in the Fenpro, need to smash and bend and make things with their hands.

I had to walk by them tearing down the building several times a day for about two months and it sucked. Denny got a new shop way up at 145th street and he hated it. It was small and isolated and pretty much the opposite of what he had before. I tried to get up there when I could and did a couple projects with him but we always had to stop after just a couple whiskies because I was on my motorcycle and he didn't have an office to crash in anymore.

He was almost done building this monster of a metal bending machine for a project when his back started hurting him so bad that Clare had to bring him in to the hospital. He had some X-rays done and then some other tests and all within a couple of hours he and Clare were told he had stage four cancer and there was no point in even admitting him. Denny told the doctor, "That's okay. I haven't been very happy lately, anyway."

I got the news he was sick and even though he didn't want anybody to see him as he was bedridden and dying, I was able to do something for him. He wanted to make sure all of his tools were sold at auction for as much as possible for Clare, and he got really upset and agitated when his friends and people that he'd worked with kept showing up at his shop to get certain tools and measuring devices of his, some of which were super cool and rare. A couple things started disappearing so I sent out a group text demanding everything be brought back immediately so it could be put up for auction along with everything else, and although it wasn't much, really, Clare said it helped calm him down and he was able to die in peace.

When Dave died (See- Dave Dies, the Scottish Buddhist Cookbook, Another Book of Mormon, Kenneth Craig Publishing Company, 2015), it was a shock that knocked me sideways and took me months to come to terms with. But with Denny, I had time to process it and do something in the end for him, so my memories of him are the fun ones. Like when he told me about the time in high school shop class when he made a pair of glasses out of a prism that, when you looked through them, up was down and down was up. We spent a few nights recreating the glasses and it was like an old school version of virtual reality. When you looked down it was the ceiling and when you looked up it was the floor. It was freaky and you looked like Bubbles from Trailer Park Boys at his drunkest when you tried to walk.

I asked him what happened to the glasses he made in high school and he said they took them away and gave him a suspension because some dumbass kid fell down some stairs and broke his leg. Denny had a ton of stories like that and as things were going to auction I really wanted to grab one of his metal shot glasses that we would drink out of, but I didn't. I thought it would be nice to have something to remind me of him when I had a whisky but it turns out I think about him all the time just fine without it.

JOB SEARCH

When I was at Ride the Ducks I got to hang out with friends and drive a WWII-era amphibious vehicle into the lake everyday. It was fun, but it was also good for me. Because I had to pass a physical every year, I had to keep my BMI under a certain level, which was incentive enough to watch what I eat, not drink so much and walk to work instead of riding my bike. But I also had to stay on top of my mental health.

For both a Coast Guard Captain's License and Commercial Drivers License you need to maintain a Medical Card that requires a physical exam. One of the things they ask you is if you're taking any medication for any kind of mental condition. I lied the first time but two years later when my card needed renewal I confessed that I was on lithium for bipolar disorder. The doctor acted like nobody had ever admitted that to him before and he had to talk to somebody about what to do. I sat there wondering if I should have continued to lie like apparently every other manic depressive with a CDL must have done. He came back and told me I had to get a letter from my psychiatrist saying I wasn't a threat to the public or my passengers. And now, instead of getting my medical card renewed every other year, I have to get it renewed every single year which is a pain in the ass because I keep it current whether I have a driving job or not.

When Ride The Ducks shut down because of the Pandemic, a few of us captains did deliveries of high-end gift baskets for Pike Place Market. It was nice to help local businesses stay alive but there's nothing more frustrating than just driving from one end of town to the other. Especially when out of forty addresses, at least ten were either entered wrong, the residence was not numbered or it just plain didn't exist. I hated this job so much that when they sent out a group email saying we'd lost the contract to FedEx, I was the only one who was openly thrilled about it. I decided to go on unemployment, which I didn't feel guilty about all because I've always worked and never drawn on it before so, if not now, when?

I had the time and money to build out my portable cabin and it was fun and I was grateful for it, but after a few months of day drinking and screwing boards together, I wanted the routine and camaraderie that comes with a real job. So I got a job as an Enumerator for the US Census. It sounded like a good deal and since trump was trying to sabotage the whole thing, it felt like I was a part of The Resistance, counting people he didn't want counted. The problem was that my neighborhood was Ballard which is mostly full of liberal white people who vote early and return their Census forms without needing a visit from a temporary federal employee. When every single person in Ballard was accounted for, which took about a month, I was sent to a certain Downtown low-income housing complex. On my first day I was about to take the elevator up to the fifth floor when the doors opened and some guy with a beer in a paper bag got off and warned me, "Somebody peed in the elevator." I took the stairs. When I got to the fifth floor unit I knocked on the door and heard somebody from behind me say, "Come on in, brother." I turned to see some fat, hairy old guy, completely naked lying on a bed. I left immediately and called it a day. That was the only nice thing about doing the Census- you got to make your own hours.

I went back to work on my portable cabin, got my unemployment going again and took up oil painting. But I still needed a real job, so I got on Indeed and started applying for the cool jobs first.

I've always been good at getting work and I knew I'd be employed again within a couple weeks, easy.

The Ketchikan version of Ride the Ducks tried to come in and fill the void left by Seattle's Ride the Ducks, which would have been perfect for me. But the City, State, US Coast Guard and almost every resident of Seattle hated the Ducks so much it was never gonna happen, which was a major pisser. I could have been Captain Braveliver again and that was all I ever really wanted.

I saw that the City was hiring a drawbridge operator so I texted Greg and told him I was available to start tomorrow and that I still had my ID, hard hat and safety vest. He told me, "There's a new hiring process now. Good luck." I had to apply online like a commoner and about a month later I was granted a zoom meeting with Mary, the head of the department. I was glad Mary was still there and figured I was as good as hired. I only worked there a year, part-time, the first time but I was reliable and never broke a drawbridge.

Also on the zoom meeting were two people I didn't know but one was from something like the Diversity Department. By the time the interview was over I knew I wasn't gonna be a drawbridge operator again. I knew where to go to look at the org chart of every department in the city and saw that of the forty drawbridge operators, two were women, one was black and three were hispanic, although one of them looked even whiter than me. I decided I should start applying for jobs as a transgender Native American because nobody would dare call me out on it.

I understand. There should be more women and people of color up on the bridges in those sweet, sweet city jobs. And maybe hiring people with no experience is the only way to achieve that. I just wish they had started doing that years ago so this wouldn't be such a problem now. Besides, it wasn't my white privilege that got me my bridge job the first time, anyway, it was nepotism.

Right after that I applied for a job to operate the two local Washington State drawbridges. The ad said 'Bridge Operator' but as soon as the interview started they explained that the job was more 'Painter of the Undersides of Freeway Bridges to Cover Graffiti and When You're Not Doing That You'll Be Painting the Tops of Drawbridges and Maybe a Couple Times a Month You'll Be Called In To Actually Operate One of the Bridges'. I must not have been able to hide my disinterest because they called to tell me that I wasn't their first choice for this position but then they threatened to call me if something else came up.

Next, I applied to be a cop with the Seattle Police Department, for the second time. It was a long process but I needed the time to get in shape. There were a bunch of tests I needed to do well on, like tests that measure reflexes, writing skills and racist beliefs. I passed all of them and was scheduled for my next two tests, which would take a full weekend. The physical test would be, get this, 20 push ups in 90 seconds, 25 sit ups in 90 seconds, and **35** squat thrusts in **3** minutes. They used to do a 1.5 mile run that had to be done in 10 minutes but they thankfully stopped because too many people were injuring themselves when they dropped from exhaustion. I practiced every day and was definitely getting in shape when I got a call from the sergeant who would be administering the psychological examination and the polygraph test. He saw that I admitted I was on lithium for my bipolar disorder and he thanked me for my honesty. I nervously told him that it was my understanding that a bipolar diagnosis was not necessarily an automatic dis-qualifier. He said that was true and gave me an example where it would be acceptable. "Let's say twenty years ago somebody suggested you might be bipolar but they didn't prescribe any medications and there have never been any incidents of erratic behavior since then…". We talked for a little bit and he said I could still come in but based on what he just heard, I really didn't stand a chance and I should consider another career. I was pretty bummed but at least I could stop doing those miserable squat thrusts.

I applied for a job with the railroad and got a call from a guy who was nice enough to tell me that I seemed like somebody who would be fun to hang out with but there was no way he would hire me because of my erratic work history. He suggested I cut my resume down to just the last three jobs that I stuck with for more than a year. We talked about bagpipes and he actually hinted that I would have a hard time getting a job if I appeared to be, you know, bipolar or something. No shit.

So I decided that if I was gonna be judged on my disorder, I may as well make it work for me. I started the process to get certified as a Peer Counselor. A few times in the past I looked into getting a job in social work but every job demanded at least a bachelor's degree. I gave up on that career path for many years and then heard about the concept of Peer Counseling, where you can use your life experience with either drug or alcohol addiction and/or your mental illness to-wards a certification without all the school work. Most of the peer counseling jobs I saw were to help get people who were homeless off the street and into housing and once I did that for a year I'd move up to Peer Navigator which is all about going around with a police officer on calls that involve somebody experiencing a mental breakdown. The beauty of this is that the peer counselor takes the lead and the cop is there in the background, gun in holster, just to provide support if needed.

I got excited about this new career and I researched who I wanted to work for. DESC kept coming up so I applied for three different positions with them. Nowadays every job application asks for your race and how you identify sexually. I admitted to being a white straight male and hoped they would offer me an interview anyway. I got a zoom interview for the first job and it was two very nice young women of color. One of their first questions was,

"Explain how you've benefited from white privilege and tell us what you've done to make up for it", or something to that effect. They dragged me along for a couple months and I couldn't help but feel that they were just keeping me on the hook in case they couldn't find somebody who checked their proper boxes. And again, I had no room to complain because I HAVE benefited from white privilege for much of my life. I did a lot of stupid shit as a teenager and was usually able to charm my way out of things that a black kid certainly would not have. Did I get jobs that a black woman with similar capabilities didn't? I don't know, but either way, my white privilege had officially run out.

I was starting to panic so I applied for so many jobs I can't remember them all. I applied to work on a party boat, even though my job would definitely involve cleaning up vomit after bachelorette parties, I was warned. I went for a job as a metal fabricator, hand adhesive applicator (odd title but an established company), personal assistant, marketing assistant, assistant at Seattle Anxiety Clinic, more peer counselor jobs, King County Property Tax Collector so I could fuck with my friends, and a couple of school bus driver jobs. The only one that got back to me was for a Christian school in Bellevue and when they asked me what religion I was (apparently they're allowed to ask that), I said I was a Scottish Buddhist but that I could work with Christians under the right circumstances.

I got a call back from the largest funeral home in Seattle about being a salesman who dresses in business casual wear and upsells coffins to the newly widowed. I tried to think of a worse job but I couldn't.

I tried to get a job as a letter press operator and had romantic notions of dressing up like an old printer and letting women in bars notice my ink covered hands and explaining the history of typesetting. Did you know that Steve Gutenberg actually IS a descendant of that other Gutenberg? Same spelling and everything!

I applied to be a Court Marshal which I guessed was in between a security guard and a police officer, but they never got back to me so I'll never know. I went for a bunch of customer service representative jobs but fortunately none of them wanted to hire me. I also applied to be a pet courier for Woof Airlines 'cause that sounded like fun. You deliver a cat to Atlanta, pick up a dog there and fly it to Germany, grab another dog and fly it to Halifax, hang out in the airport for a couple days and get a cat to fly to Vegas, then a dog to fly to Fairbanks, and from there deliver another dog home to Seattle. I could think of so many ways this job could suck but I was seriously getting desperate now. They didn't hire me.

I had high hopes for the next potential job- Light Rail Operator. I love all forms of mass transit and being a Train Conductor would check off another box in my quest to operate every large piece of movable machinery and vehicle in Seattle. If I could be Train Conductor for a little while that would only leave the Ballard Locks but that would never happen because I was told years ago that you have to be a member of the Army Corps of Engineers and once you're in there you don't have a say in where you're stationed. You could end up in goddamn Louisiana. I thought my interview went well but I must have come across as too eager and I realized I may never be a train conductor.

There were a few writing jobs I applied for, namely writing a column for PNW Magazine that I would have been horrible at but at least it would look good on my resume. And then one night I was trying to figure out how stone columns were made. Particularly the ones on all the buildings built after the Great Seattle Fire. They certainly didn't carve them in place, and with all those buildings going up at once there had to be at least one good sized factory that could handle making all those pillars, but I couldn't find any mention of it. My guess is that as soon as a delivery of sandstone or limestone came into the job site, a bunch would get sent off to the column factory. And the only way I could see these perfect pillars being made would be to turn them on a big ass lathe. And if you want to see something impressive, look at John Parkinson's Interurban Building (See- Pioneer Square Walking Tour, #11). It's an amazing building but notice the columns. They're turned brick! I wanted to know how columns were made, even going all the way back to the Greeks. How did they get them so smooth by hand? I couldn't find much online so I thought maybe I could find some old mason who knew all this stuff. Pioneer Masonry in Ballard kept coming up and I knew them from seeing their signage on all the big restoration projects around town. I saw that they had a page on their site for Careers and could totally see myself up on some scaffolding cleaning a gargoyle with a toothbrush. I talked to somebody and he was gonna get back to me but he never did. Probably wouldn't have been as much fun as I thought it would be anyway.

I saw that the Ballard Locks is hiring civilians now, incredibly. I didn't get my hopes up when I applied but I couldn't help but think it would be the perfect job for me. Just showing up for work and walking through the English Gardens (which aren't British, by the way, they were created by a guy named Carl English) and over the gates to start my day would be wonderful. I had a good phone interview, I thought, and when they asked that question that I'm never prepared for even though so many of them ask it, I kind of choked. "What would you say is your biggest weakness?", like anybody would ever answer that honestly. 'I may drink too much'? 'Relationships scare me'? 'Math'? Is there even a right answer to this question? So I said, "Well, I can get really excited about things and people tell me it can be annoying...". They told me they'd get back to me in two weeks and when they didn't, I felt like I couldn't call them because I wanted to show that I wasn't overexcited about the job and a couple months later they sent me an email telling me I didn't get it.

Several months after that I re-applied and got offered the job as a Lock and Dam Operator but turned it down because the schedule looked horrible. There were 8 hour rotating shifts (they run 24 hours, 365 days a year) but also something called a 5-4-9 shift and I didn't even WANT to know what was. Ten or twenty years ago, sure, but not at fifty-seven. It was nice they asked, I said, but no thank you.

I then applied to drive those red double-decker hop on, hop off buses. At least they seem to be more desperate than me so that was a good sign. I thought it would be a good gig for the tourist season, just driving the same route, probably, and getting my max 60 hours of driving time in every week. By mid-September I'd have enough money so I could go to Scotland for a couple weeks, finally. They hired me immediately and my entire training was done in less than a day, which was concerning. The next day was our opening day and the bus I was given had the right front mirror held up with a wine cork and two different colors of duct tape. A passenger flipped out on me because it started down-pouring and there was no place for people on the top deck to go because the bottom level was oversold and he kept yelling 'People are dying!!' in my ear while I tried to navigate this probably-not-even-legal piece of shit back to the hop on spot next to the Space Needle. On the next trip I had to switch buses with the other driver for some unmentioned reason which I figured out five minutes later when the front end bottomed out going down Broad Street and the other driver threatened to quit if he ever had to drive that particular piece of shit again. I quit that night by text and applied for a job taking people up Mt Rainier.

It was one of those companies that for a couple hundred bucks will pick you and a few other couples up at your hotels, stop and serve some French press coffee and healthy pastries, do a couple grueling but amazing hikes in the snow, then make a fancy lunch and have another nature walk. It was a great job for college kids on their summer break because they could make a couple bucks while showing off their botany knowledge, but not so much for an old guy like me who needed real money and didn't want to have to hide his heavy breathing while taking his snow shoes off, so of course I quit.

I went up to a friend's lake cabin at the end of a long logging road outside Port Townsend to do some work, and as much as I liked fixing up a cool cabin without electricity and installing a Craigger, I would go days without seeing anybody. All there was to do at night was stare into a fire and think about things, which is okay a couple times but it's nothing a manic depressive should ever make a habit of. So I went into town and checked Indeed for my next job. I tried to think of someplace cool that I could walk to and be around a lot of people when I remembered Seattle Center.

Seattle Center is the current site for what was 1962's Century 21 Exposition, aka the Seattle World's Fair. It was actually held in honor of Seattle's first World's Fair, the Alaskan-Yukon-Pacific Exposition of 1909, which was held in honor of the Klondike Gold Rush. All three events brought countless people and their money to Seattle and this city would not be what it is without any one of them. Or Elmer Fisher, for that matter.

Elmer Fisher rebuilt Seattle after the Great Fire and those buildings were used to promote Seattle as the major city in the Pacific Northwest during the Gold Rush. The A-Y-P Expo promoted Alaska and trade with the Pacific Rim and left as its legacy much of the campus of the University of Washington. The 1962 World's Fair established Seattle as a pioneer in future technology as well as leaving behind some legacies of its own, namely the Space Needle and the Monorail.

The Seattle Monorail was built to move visitors from their hotels Downtown to the Expo without clogging up the streets. Millions of people were so eager to ride the monorail that the whole thing paid for itself in just a couple months. After the fair, people kept riding it because it's a fun way to get Downtown from Seattle Center and it's faster than the twenty minute walk or the buses.

Working at the Monorail seemed like a natural next job for me, so I applied and had a zoom meeting from the isolated cabin outside of Port Townsend and got the job to be a Train Conductor, although they call it Driver/CSR because it's cheaper. It's fun and it's kind of perfect for me in many ways- there's a set schedule, something monotonous that requires my full attention because there's always the possibility of something happening, and lots of people to interact with.

I know that I will always work, it is as much my therapy as a means of survival. I won't always be with the Monorail, but I know that I will always have to have a job. All I need is the right one.